A Heritage
of Col

Natural Dyes Past

Published in Great Britain 2014 by
Search Press Limited
Wellwood, North Farm Road,
Tunbridge Wells, Kent TN2 3DR

ISBN: 978–1–78221–036–8

The author has made every effort to ensure that all the
information and instructions given in this book are accurate and
safe, but the author cannot accept liability, whether direct or
consequential and however arising, for any injuries, losses or other
damages resulting from the use of information in this book.

The author also wishes to point out that the shades on the colour
samples and photographs may not be a true representation because
of the limitations of colour reproduction.

Printed in China

A Heritage of Colour
Natural Dyes Past and Present

JENNY DEAN

Search Press

CONTENTS

Introduction

When I made my first dye bath nearly forty years ago, little did I realise that I was about to embark on a fascinating journey of discovery that would take me in so many different directions. As a beginner, I followed instructions and recipes without question, hoping to obtain the colours that seemed to be promised. From the many unexpected results and the occasional disappointment that this approach brought, I gradually realised that nothing should be taken for granted and that one should always learn from one's own experiences, rather than relying on the experiences of others. From this grew my delight in experimentation and the joy of discovering the remarkable colour secrets of the plant world.

As time passed, I also began to feel that many aspects of natural dyeing might benefit from closer examination, especially in the light of the environmental and safety concerns that have assumed such great importance during the last decades. So I began to attempt to address issues such as: Do dyers really need to use so many manufactured chemicals? Must all dyes be applied with heat? Can we use water more economically? Should we rely so much on imported dyestuffs or can we make more use of what is around us and what we can grow? And last but by no means least: What can we learn from the dyers of the more distant past, who created beautiful colours without the use of manufactured chemicals?

The issue of man-made chemicals concerns many dyers and in recent years the quantities of manufactured chemicals recommended for use in natural dyeing have decreased. Most dyers today probably use aluminium sulphate (alum) as their preferred mordant – a substance used to help fix dye colour to the fibres – and may use iron and copper sulphates, either as colour modifiers after dyeing or sometimes as mordants, but the use of chrome is becoming rarer and tin, too, is used less frequently. There is also an increased interest in alternative fixatives, such as plant tannins, and some dyers prefer to use only dyes that can be applied successfully without the need for a mordant or fixative at all.

Use of the term "eco-dyeing" has become common among dyers and it goes without saying that natural dyeing should always be carried out with concern for the environment and with careful use of natural resources. It may, for example, become more desirable for dyers to limit their use of heat and water, at least as much as is feasible for successful dyeing. Many dyes can be applied without heating the dye bath and although leaving dye pots in sunny positions can be helpful, good results can often be achieved without any warmth at all. It is also possible to make heat-retaining insulated containers for dye pots, which can then be left for as long as necessary to allow the dye colour to develop on the fibres gradually. Dye and mordant solutions can often be stored and re-used, and collected rain water or sea water can be used instead of water from the household tap.

As far as selecting dyes is concerned, by making use of what is around them and using mainly locally sourced dyestuffs, dyers can obtain a wide range of colours without the need for imported dyes. However, although this may be environmentally desirable as it reduces the need for transport by air, it is also important to remember that many imported dyes come from managed sources and provide income for people who may have few other opportunities for earning a living, so using imported dyestuffs can have positive implications too. Also, some imported dyes give colours that may be difficult to achieve from native dyes.

It was in part my interest in learning from the textile techniques of the more distant past that led me to start investigating the dyes and methods of Iron Age and early Anglo-Saxon dyers. Unfortunately, textiles generally tend to decay and perish relatively quickly, so very little remains to provide evidence of the dyes and working methods of these early dyers. However, scientific investigation and technical analysis of the few textile fragments and textile-related artefacts available for study provide much valuable information and this enabled me to embark on my most recent series of experiments. The results of these experiments were the starting point for this book.

My aim is to show what can be achieved using dyes harvested locally or grown in the garden and with minimal use of manufactured chemicals. This book is not intended as a recipe book for achieving specific colours from the dye plants featured but rather as an illustration of the considerable potential for obtaining a wide range of colours from whatever plant materials each dyer may have available. The emphasis is on methods of experimentation and the techniques described here to prepare and process the dyestuffs can be applied to the dye materials each dyer finds locally. So, for example, the methods used to extract colour from buckthorn bark or willow bark can be applied to barks from other trees and the cool dyeing methods used for rhubarb root or madder can be used experimentally with other plants.

The dye pot can often produce exciting and unexpected results, as I have discovered during my investigations into the world of natural colour, and there is still much to learn. I hope, through this book, to share with others my love of experimentation and to encourage craftspeople the world over to experience for themselves the thrill of exploring the colour potential of the plants around them.

Inspiration from the Past

For several years I have been conducting experiments based on the dyes and techniques available to dyers of the past. When we moved from Bedfordshire to West Sussex in the south of England, chance brought us to the village of Findon in the South Downs. Findon lies at the foot of Cissbury Ring, an Iron Age hill fort whose early inhabitants left archaeological evidence to indicate that textile production had been carried out on the site. So it seems fitting that my interests as a dyer have led me to investigate the dyes and methods which might have been used by people who lived and worked in this same area so many years ago.

On top of Cissbury Ring

I had already investigated the dyes used by the early Anglo-Saxons and when I was asked to lead a workshop on "Colours of the Celts", I started to search for information about the dyes and techniques that might have been used by the Celts.

The word "Celt" derived from the Greek word "keltoi", meaning any foreigner, and was first used by Roman historians and geographers, who applied the term to tribes they encountered in Continental Europe. It is generally used to describe tribal societies in Iron Age and Roman-era Europe, who spoke Celtic languages and were loosely tied by similar language, religion and cultural expression.

My research led me first to the archaeological reports on the textile fragments discovered at the Iron Age site at Hallstatt in Austria. The

Hallstatt culture (c. 800 BCE–450 BCE), named after the site of the rich grave finds at Hallstatt, was the proto-Celtic culture in Europe. This culture then spread over much of Europe, into Britain, France, Central Europe, the Iberian Peninsula and Northern Italy. The conditions in the salt mines, where the graves were discovered, meant that the textiles found there were relatively well preserved and analysis carried out on them gives an indication of some of the dyes and techniques probably used by the Hallstatt Celts.

The textile fragments from Hallstatt still show clear evidence of some of their colours. Blue from woad and yellow from weld were identified and also tannin, although it was not possible to identify the precise source of this tannin. Other unidentified yellow dyes were found, possibly from saw-wort or chamomile, and there is evidence that the purple dye obtainable from some species of lichens was also used. All these dyes were probably from plants grown or harvested in the local area.

The red dyes analysed are interesting. There was no trace of any of the madder-type sources of red, which one might have expected, but some indication of unidentified insect dyes, possibly Polish or Armenian cochineal, and of kermes, also a red dye from insects. This suggests that the red dyes – or perhaps the textiles dyed with them – were probably imported from elsewhere, as it is unlikely that the dyes mentioned would have been available locally. Both white and naturally-pigmented wool was dyed and there is evidence of over-dyeing to create further shades.

Iron and copper were identified on several fragments and aluminium was also found, but on fewer fragments. However, it is possible that these minerals were present as a result of contamination within the salt mine, rather than because they were intentionally used in dyeing. This seems probable, as the situations in which the aluminium, iron and copper residues were found do not necessarily indicate their systematic use in dyeing, except where iron may have been used in combination with tannin to create dark grey and black. It is difficult to know whether mineral alum would have been available to the Iron Age Celts for use as a mordant, especially in Britain. Alum shale was not discovered in Britain until the seventeenth century and for several centuries prior to that alum was imported into Britain, mainly from Italy, Spain and Asia Minor. However, whilst it is not impossible, it would seem unlikely that mineral alum would have been readily available in Britain as early as the Iron Age. Aluminium can also be extracted from some plants, for example clubmosses, and this may perhaps have been done by some Iron Age Celtic peoples. However, iron and copper could have been used, either in the form of iron and copper solutions (made by soaking pieces of iron or copper in vinegar and water), or perhaps by adding pieces of metal to the dye bath or by using dye vessels made from iron or copper. Also, tannin from various sources may have been used as a mordant or base for other colours or added to dye baths, perhaps to improve colour fastness.

For the initial experiments I carried out in preparation for the workshop, I used both white and naturally coloured light brown and grey wool and treated some samples in a tannin solution (from oak bark) before dyeing them. The remaining samples were unmordanted.

I based my selection of dyes on the results of the analysis of the Hallstatt textiles and also on information from other archaeological finds from the period. The dyes I used were woad (*Isatis tinctoria*), which seems to have been used for blues throughout Europe from early times, weld (*Reseda luteola*) for yellows, and for reds I used wild madder (*Rubia peregrina*) and bedstraws (*Galium spp.*), which were used for reds before dyer's madder (*Rubia tinctorum*) began to be imported and then cultivated in Europe. I also used purple from the lichen *Ochrolechia tartarea* and tannin from oak bark.

The results of these experiments were interesting and indicated that bright, clear colours could be achieved with many dyes without an alum mordant. In addition, the use of tannin as a base for other colours seemed to be a technique possibly used by the Celts and so I decided to experiment further along these lines, without using man-made chemicals as a pre-mordant.

Some of the results from a Celtic dye workshop

I also looked for further information about other early textile fragments and it would seem that the most frequently used dyes in Britain and many other parts of Europe were woad, madder (or related plants such as wild madder and bedstraws), weld and dyer's broom. These classic dyes are still widely used today and this book is, in part, a celebration of the versatility of these remarkable sources of colour.

Recent research indicates that during the Iron Age, in areas of Scandinavia where madder and madder-related plants were not readily available, reds may have been obtained from tannin-rich barks, such as buckthorn bark. Technical analysis of the red colours on some wool fragments from an Iron Age burial in Finland provides evidence for this, as the results of this analysis show that these fragments contain tannins but bear no traces of madder-type dyes. This suggests that the red colour may have come from tree bark. The possibility of obtaining reds from the bark of trees, without the use of a mordant, intrigued me and led to many experiments, especially with the alkaline colour extraction method (page 32) and buckthorn bark.

As my experiments progressed, it gradually became clear that the alkaline extraction method might be an excellent way of achieving strong colours without heat from a range of dyes, simply by soaking fibres and dyestuff in a cool alkaline solution for a day or two. It certainly seemed likely that this method could have been used by early dyers, who would have needed only to add water to the cold ashes collected from their wood fires and then to leave the mixture to steep for a while, in order to create an alkaline solution for a dye bath with, for example, weld or wild madder.

As I began to expand the scope of my experiments beyond those specifically for the Celtic dye workshop, I intended initially to limit the dyes I used to those from British native plants (or those non-native plants naturalised at an early date). When I then considered extending my tests even further, it seemed a good idea to also include especially useful dye plants easily cultivated in gardens or readily found in the wild, even though not all of these are native plants.

In Britain, a true native plant is any plant that was here before the formation of the English Channel about 8000 years ago and the London Natural History Museum website provides a list of these native plants and also native plants for each UK postcode. No doubt similar information exists for native plants in other countries. Many other plants were introduced at an early date – for example woad, which was probably introduced from the Middle East by the earliest farmers in the Neolithic period. Similarly, dyer's madder (*Rubia tinctorum*) is not native but was cultivated here from the early Middle Ages and perhaps even earlier.

I had two main reasons for limiting the dyes I used. Firstly, the use of native plants or those grown in the garden or found in the wild seemed environmentally desirable from the point of view of making use of readily available dye sources, rather than using dyestuffs imported from other countries. The postcode-related native plant list also enabled me to discover which dye plants would have been available to the early dyers living in my local area at the Iron Age hill fort on Cissbury Ring and I was attracted by the idea that I could gather or grow plants that had such a special local connection. To me, there is a real thrill in being able to use dyes and techniques that might have been used more than 2000 years ago by people who trod the same earth as I now do.

My other reason was a practical one. My new dye garden is very small, so I had to limit the number of dye plants I could grow. I decided to grow only native dye plants plus, of course, dyer's madder (*Rubia tinctorum*), which is my favourite dye and one which is indispensable to me. I also included one or two other non-native plants which are particularly useful to dyers – for example rhubarb, dahlias and buddleia.

Some workshop samples dyed with madder (reds, pinks and browns), woad (blues) and weld (yellows and greens) drying in the sun

As wool is the "native" fibre for the British Isles, I limited my experiments mainly to wool. Also, wool is particularly appropriate for a resident of Findon village, as each year on the village green we have a Sheep Fair which has been held annually in Findon since the thirteenth century. Although sheep are only exhibited and are no longer bought and sold at the fair, the sight on the village green of so many sheep of a wide variety of breeds provides yet another link with the past.

Shetland sheep at Findon Sheep Fair with Jacob sheep in the background

I also added some naturally pigmented light brown and grey wool skeins to the dye baths, as these natural fleece colours produce lovely shades when over-dyed. Hand-spinners should have no difficulty in finding grey and brown fleece to spin; otherwise, ready-spun naturally coloured woollen yarns are now widely available from shops or on the internet.

From left to right: madder (NM, Gr.NM); woad (NM, Gr.NM); rhubarb root (NM, Gr.NM)

Fibres spun from flax and hemp were also used by early peoples but not frequently dyed.

The aim of my experiments was to ascertain whether it would be possible to achieve a range of bright colours without using alum as a pre-mordant and using tannin as a base or alternative plant mordant. In addition, I added an alum-mordanted sample for purposes of comparison and I also added samples of wool treated with aluminium from clubmoss to some of the dye baths.

What follows in this book is largely based on the results of the tests I carried out and the implications they may have for dyers today. Whilst many dyers will, like me, continue to use alum as a pre-mordant wherever the fastness of a dyed colour might otherwise be compromised, the potential for achieving a wide range of colours without using manufactured chemicals is considerable. I hope that the information in this book will help dyers to make informed choices about the dyes and methods they decide to use in the future and may inspire them to experiment further with the plants around them.

A view across the Sussex Downs from Cissbury Ring

Environmental Considerations

Today's natural dyers are probably more environmentally aware than the dyers of both the distant and the more recent past. Very few contemporary dyers still use chrome as a mordant and many no longer use tin. Some dyers are also questioning the use of other chemicals, such as copper, and many would like to be able to dispense with man-made chemicals altogether. To me, it has always seemed illogical to choose to use natural dyes and then to apply them by using highly toxic chemicals such as chrome. However, the need for light-fast and wash-fast colours, which are also bright and deep, remains an important consideration. My aim in this book is to demonstrate what can be achieved without chemicals, other than those occurring naturally in plants or made from wood ash and scrap iron or copper. By limiting the use of chemicals and re-using solutions wherever possible, we are less likely to harm the earth or the environment by discarding the remains of potentially harmful substances.

Water is becoming ever more precious as seasons become drier in many parts of the world and drought is an increasing threat. Dyers need to be aware of this and to consider how water can be used more economically. Rain water provides an excellent source of water for dyeing and should always be collected if possible. For dyers who live near the coast, sea water provides an alternative source of water and, at least in my experience, sea water does not generally have a significant effect on the colours produced in the dye pot. One way of using less water for dyeing is to put the fibres and dyestuff into the pot together, rather than simmering the dyestuff first to extract the colour. This method gives good results with most dyes, although it may be advisable to tie the dyestuff into a fine-meshed net or bag first, so that the dye pieces don't become entangled in the fibres, making it difficult to remove them after dyeing. Also, to ensure the fibres take up the dye evenly, they should be moved around regularly in the dye liquid, otherwise the fibres resting on the bag of dyestuff may absorb more dye colour and become a deeper shade. I also sometimes save the residues of dye baths and re-use them as the base for the next dye bath. These residues don't necessarily have to be used with the same dyestuff, as long as the second dyestuff gives a similar shade to the first one. So I may use the residues of one yellow dye bath, from weld for example, as the base for a dye bath from another yellow dye which gives similar shades of yellow, for example dyer's broom.

Selecting a source of heat is another aspect of dyeing that requires consideration. Energy, from electricity, oil or gas for example, is precious and also expensive, so it may be desirable wherever feasible to select dyes that can be applied without heat - and many can, although patience may be required for full colours to develop. If it is possible to dye in the open air, then using a fire made with wood scavenged from the wild or from other people's cast-offs may be an option. Outside houses one can often find useful waste wood awaiting disposal and the householder may be only too happy for this wood to be taken. It is also possible to heat different dyes in one large dye vessel, if several heatproof preserving jars, each containing water, fibres and dyestuff, are heated in a single large pan of water. There are also ways of enabling dye baths to retain heat, such as using a solar oven or an insulated box.

As far as sourcing dyestuffs is concerned, a wide range of colours is available from wild or garden plants, which are generally free of charge. It is against the law to uproot any plants growing in the wild but the careful dyer should have no difficulty in gathering moderate amounts of leaves, flowers and shoots from wild plants without harming the plants in question, although permission must always be obtained before collecting anything from private property. Weld, for example, often springs up by the roadside, only to be cut down later by local authority workers. As long as the dyer leaves some flowering shoots to self-seed, harvesting some of this wild weld should be perfectly acceptable.

It is generally considered environmentally desirable to avoid using too many dyes that have been imported from abroad. However, some dyes can only be obtained in this way and many of these are from managed sources and the trade provides valuable work and income.

Flower dead-heads, especially of buddleia and dahlias, provide useful sources of colour and gardening friends are usually happy to save dead-heads for dyers or would welcome the enthusiastic dyer willing to do the dead-heading in exchange for the flower heads. Some important dyes, for example madder for reds and a source of indigo blue such as woad, are not difficult to grow. For dyers without access to a garden, most of the important native dyes can be bought from suppliers, while indigo in powder form is also readily available to provide blues.

The issue of whether or not to use manufactured chemicals, such as alum or iron and copper sulphates, is one which each individual dyer must consider in the light of personal preferences and the projects for which the dyed materials are intended. For the dyer who wishes to use no additional chemicals other than home-made wood ash water and perhaps iron water, it is still possible to achieve a wide range of colours, although these colours may not always be as rich or as bright as those achieved on alum-mordanted materials and some may be less fast to light and washing.

Although it may be tempting to dispense with manufactured chemicals altogether, the dyer must remain aware of the importance of light-fastness and wash-fastness, especially if producing items for sale. My personal motto is: "If in doubt, use an alum mordant". Conducting one's own tests for fastness is the only way to know whether a dye applied in a particular way will have the necessary degrees of fastness for a specific project. Fastness requirements can vary according to the project in which the dyed materials are to be used. For example: a wall hanging or furnishing fabric, which will be exposed to light for prolonged periods, would require a high level of light-fastness but wash-fastness would be of less importance for a wall hanging than for furnishing fabrics.

Although in this book the focus is frequently on what we can learn from the dyeing methods of the past, it would also seem sensible not to ignore some of the more useful substances available to the dyers of today. I would personally not wish to dispense completely with alum as a mordant and it is worth noting that, once alum became available to the dyers of the past, its value was recognised immediately; it rapidly became an important commodity of trade and its use became widespread. Whilst it may be preferable to avoid the use of highly toxic substances, such as chrome, which can harm both humans and the environment, chemicals such as alum and iron, if used with care and disposed of safely, should pose little threat to humans or to the environment and can enable dyers to produce a wide range of deep, fast colours. Also, if one opts to use chemicals such as alum sulphate and iron and copper sulphates or waters, it is possible to store the solutions and re-use them, so the need to dispose of chemical solutions is very much reduced. If appropriate quantities of mordant are used and correctly applied, there should be little or no chemical residues remaining in the solution anyway.

As always, each dyer will need to select the dyes and methods which are most appropriate to his or her particular situation and requirements. The important thing is to have the necessary knowledge and experience to make informed choices. As long as dyers remain alert to the human and environmental implications of the materials they use and the techniques they employ, no harm should come to humans or to the natural world, which provides us with the raw materials for creating such a rich array of glorious colours.

NB: The key to the abbreviations used for the dyed samples in the photographs is on page 48.

The Basics

Equipment
Label each item clearly as dyeing equipment and do not use the same equipment for food preparation.

You will need:

• at least two heatproof pots able to hold 14–18 litres (3–4 gallons) of liquid. Stainless steel or heatproof glass is best but enamelled or aluminium pots can also be used, although they are more difficult to clean after use and solutions containing washing soda can damage aluminium. Each pot should preferably have a lid
• three or four smaller heatproof pots, also preferably with lids. Again, stainless steel or heatproof glass is best
• several plastic bowls or buckets, some with lids, for soaking dyestuffs and fibres, for rinsing and for storing liquids. A large lidded plastic bucket can also be useful for solutions that don't require heating. Large glass jars and plastic containers with lids are very handy for storing liquids or for cool dye baths
• stainless steel tongs, long-handled spoons or strong wooden or heatproof plastic rods for stirring liquids and removing materials from the dye pot
• a heatproof glass or plastic measuring jug
• a set of measuring spoons
• weighing scales, preferably calibrated in grammes
• a wire mesh strainer for straining off finely chopped dyestuffs
• a larger strainer or colander for straining off other dyestuffs. A strainer that will sit on the top of a pot or bucket, without having to be held, is especially useful, as it leaves the hands free for holding the hot dye pot
• rubber gloves, preferably with a cotton lining
• a plastic-backed apron
• oven gloves or pot holders
• a dust-mask for use when dealing with fine powders
• a dairy or scientific thermometer is useful but not essential
• a heat source
• a source of water
• pH papers to check the pH values of water and dye baths
• cleaning materials
• labels for identifying skeins etc. after dyeing
• two or three funnels in different sizes for use when pouring mordant or dye solutions into bottles for storage.

Dyers in the past would have used pots made of iron and possibly copper. There is no reason why pots made from these metals should not be used by the dyers of today. They may sometimes have an effect on the dye colours produced, but some dyers regard this as an advantage.

An old iron cooking pot that could be used for dyeing

pH values
It is a good idea to check the pH value of the water you use for dyeing and to know how to make adjustments if necessary. The best way to do this is to purchase a roll of pH test paper or a booklet of pH papers, either from a pharmacist or from a specialist dyestuff supplier. When dipped in water the pH paper will change colour. The colour can then be compared with the colours on the chart supplied with the papers. This will give you a pH reading. A value of pH7 is neutral; anything below 7 becomes increasingly acidic and anything above 7 becomes increasingly alkaline. Neutral water is usually considered best for dyeing but water with a pH value of between 5.5 and 8.5 is unlikely to significantly affect the majority of dye colours.

Adjusting the pH value of your water or dye bath is easy. To make your water more alkaline, add a very small amount of an alkali and then re-test. Keep doing this until you get the reading you need. Sources of alkali include washing soda, soda ash, wood ash water (see page 35) and ground chalk or limestone.

To make your water more acidic, add a few drops of clear vinegar (5% acetic acid) or lemon juice or a few citric acid crystals. Then re-test and if necessary continue to gradually add more clear vinegar, lemon juice or citric acid until you achieve the desired reading.

Selecting and Preparing Fibres for Dyeing

The choice of fibres to dye will be a personal one. I have selected wool as my fibre of choice, as this is my "native" fibre and this book is partly about making use of native and local resources. However, there is no reason why the dyes featured should not be applied to other animal (or protein) fibres, such as silk, alpaca and mohair, and also to vegetable (or cellulose) fibres, such as cotton, linen and hemp. Where they differ from the details for wool, instructions for preparing and dyeing other fibres are also given below.

Sussex-bred alpacas with fleece in several colours

Dyed alpaca samples

For most of my experiments I used wool in a selection of natural shades of white, light grey and light brown. Naturally pigmented wool in shades of fawn, brown and grey can give lovely colours when dyed and nowadays it is not difficult to purchase naturally pigmented wool in skeins or as fibres for hand-spinning. If samples of grey and brown wool are added to dye baths, the colour range from each dye can be extended further.

Dyeing lengths of fabric and pieces of cloth

The dyes and dyeing methods described in this book can be used on both skeins of yarn and lengths of fabric or pieces of cloth. Yarns are sometimes simpler to dye because they are more compact in the dye pot and more readily absorb the dye colour evenly. Fabrics and cloth need plenty of space to move freely in the solution and should be gently moved around in the dye pot from time to time, in order to ensure even penetration of the mordant or dye and to avoid patchy dyeing. Otherwise, the methods are exactly the same for both yarns and fabric lengths or pieces of cloth.

Cleaning Fibres for Dyeing

NB: Always wear rubber gloves when handling raw unwashed fibres.

It is important to first make a note of the dry weight of whatever you intend to dye. This saves much frustration later on, when you have washed or wetted out the materials ready for the dye pot, only to remember too late that they should be dry before they are weighed. Before mordanting or dyeing, all fibres, whether bought as ready-for-dyeing or not, must be completely clean and free from any grease or dirt that may impede the penetration of the mordant or dye. Scouring agent, which is a cleanser used in the wool industry, can be purchased from specialist suppliers but dishwashing liquid can also be used as a cleanser.

Cleaning animal fibres (e.g. wool, silk, alpaca, mohair)

Use about 1 teaspoon of dishwashing liquid or a ½ teaspoon of scouring agent per 7 litres (1½ gallons) of water. If you are using raw, unspun fleece or yarns spun from unwashed fleece, these should first be soaked for 6–12 hours, or overnight, in the cleaning solution. Don't use very hot water as this may cause delicate fibres to felt and don't stir or squeeze the fibres in the solution. If the materials are very dirty and greasy, change the water and add more cleanser after about 3–4 hours. Then remove the materials and rinse them in warm, but not hot, water. Wash them again and rinse very thoroughly several times.

If you are using silk which has not been degummed, this should be gradually heated in the cleaning solution. Heat it slowly to just below a simmer and keep it at this temperature for 30–60 minutes. Do not allow it to boil. If the silk still feels sticky, you may need to repeat the process. Then rinse very thoroughly several times.

Other wool and silk materials and other animal fibres should be washed well and then rinsed very thoroughly several times.

Cleaning vegetable fibres (e.g. cotton, linen, hemp)

Vegetable fibres should be gently simmered for about 2 hours in a solution of cleanser and washing soda. Use 1 teaspoon of dishwashing liquid or a ½ teaspoon of scouring agent plus 2–3 teaspoons of washing soda per 7 litres (1½ gallons) of water.

Cotton contains wax, oil and pectic substances and the water will become brown as these are washed out. It is often a good idea to wash cotton twice, rinsing very well between washes and making a fresh cleaning solution for the second wash. Then rinse very thoroughly several times.

Selecting, Harvesting and Preparing Dyes

The choice of dye depends primarily, of course, on the colour one wishes to achieve. Other considerations include whether the selected dye has the degree of fastness necessary for the planned project. As I don't always have a particular project in mind, I try to ensure that all the materials I dye will be as light-fast and wash-fast as possible. This means that I tend mainly to use a limited number of dyes which I know are reliable, including traditional dyes such as madder, weld, dyer's broom, woad, walnut and buckthorn and tannin-rich dyes from the barks of various trees.

Yellow and tan colours are available from many plant sources, so dyers should have plenty of choice where these colours are concerned.

For red shades the sources are more limited, so madder and related plants, such as the bedstraws, tend to be indispensable, as does buckthorn bark, which can also be used for reds.

The only traditional British source of blue is indigo from woad (*Isatis tinctoria*), although blue can also be obtained from *Indigofera spp.* (usually available commercially in powder form) or from home-grown Japanese Indigo (*Persicaria tinctoria*, formerly known as *Polygonum tinctorium*).

Walnut leaves drying

Weld harvested for the dye pot

Oak leaves drying

Gathering and Drying Dyestuffs

It is advisable to wear strong gloves when gathering dyestuffs, as some plants are poisonous and some have sharp thorns. Remember that bark should only be stripped from fallen or officially removed branches, as taking bark from living trees can seriously harm them. However, some trees, such as eucalyptus, shed their bark naturally. Leaves should be gathered from several different branches and not all from the same part of the tree. If you collect flowers in the wild, always leave some flowers to seed for the next crop. Also, in Britain it is against the law to uproot any plant growing in the wild, so roots cannot be harvested from the wild.

The time of year at which plant parts are collected for dyeing can have an effect on the colours produced, so leaves harvested in May will not necessarily give the same shades as leaves collected from the same tree in September. Also, different parts of the same plant will often tend to give different colours, so keep the flowers and leaves of each plant separate, unless the recipe indicates that the whole plant top should be used.

Bark shed from a eucalyptus tree

Buckthorn leaves drying

Dyer's chamomile flowers drying

Fallen autumn leaves

Dyestuffs bought from a supplier are usually dried and ready to use. If you harvest your own dyestuffs and you don't intend to use them immediately, they will need to be dried and then stored. Most gathered dyestuffs should first be cut or chopped into the smallest pieces possible. However, flowers and leaves can be dried whole and if the leaves are large they can usually be crumbled for the dye pot when they have dried completely.

If you have a very large quantity of any dyestuff that needs to be cut up, a garden shredder can be very useful. The chopped dyestuffs should be spread in a single layer on a sheet of paper and left in a dark, dry place, preferably where air can circulate around them, until they have completely dried out. I usually put dyestuffs on sheets of newspaper placed on top of wire mesh and then leave them under a bed until they are dry and ready to store.

When dry, store the dyestuffs in clearly labelled brown paper bags in a cool, dry place away from the light. Avoid using plastic bags to store dyes, as some dyestuffs can become mouldy if they absorb moisture. However, if any dyestuffs do develop mould, they should still be effective in the dye pot, although they may not necessarily give the same shades as dyestuffs without mould.

Dried bearberry (uva-ursi) leaves

Dried dahlia flower heads

Dried buckthorn bark

Dried dyer's broom

Quantities to use

Much depends, of course, on the depth of colour required but, in general, most natural plant dyes are used at the rate of 100% dyestuff, which means that one would use the same weight of dyestuff as dry weight of the materials to be dyed. However, with some plant dyes, if one is not using an alum mordant it may be advisable to use a higher percentage of dyestuff. Suggested quantities are given in the section on individual dyes. (See also notes on page 49.)

These quantities are given as a percentage per 100g (4oz) dry weight of fibres to be dyed. So 100% means 100g (4oz) dyestuff per 100g (4oz) dry weight of fibres, 50% means 50g (2oz) dyestuff per 100g (4oz) dry weight of fibres and so on. To calculate exact quantities it is best to use the metric system.

Using the percentage system for measuring

The percentage system is the most accurate measuring method, especially for small quantities of mordant chemicals. However, it does mean you need to use metric scales and measuring jugs, rather than equipment calibrated in pounds, ounces or pints. The metric system is easy to use: 2% means you need 2g per 100g dry weight of materials being treated; 10% means 10g per 100g; 25% means 25g per 100g and so on. So if your fibres weigh 250g and the mordant is used at the rate of 2% you would need to use 5g. If the mordant is used at 10%, you would need 25g for 250g of fibres. And so on. For ease of calculation, awkward weights of fibres can be rounded up to the nearest 50g, so 487g would become 500g.

For dyers without access to metric scales, approximate equivalents for small quantities are given in level teaspoons wherever possible. If you measure in teaspoons, always use the same teaspoon, preferably a 5ml teaspoon, and level off the surface with a knife.

NB: The percentages that you will see given for each plant are for fibres that have not been mordanted with alum. For alum-mordanted fibres reduce the amount of dyestuff by about 20%.

Health and Safety

Guidelines for health and safety are given on page 153.
It is important to read these guidelines very carefully before embarking on any dyeing projects.

Mordants

A mordant is a substance that acts as a bond between the fibres being dyed and the dyestuff being applied. The most common mordants are metallic salts of aluminium, iron or copper.

Always wear rubber gloves when handling mordants, as some are irritants and a few are poisonous. Wear a face mask to avoid inhaling any fine powders and keep a lid on pots when mordanting to avoid inhaling any fumes. Mordants are best applied before the fibres are dyed and mordanted fibres can be stored indefinitely. Many dyes, usually those rich in tannins, will fix without the use of a manufactured chemical mordant. Some dyers may prefer to avoid the use of manufactured chemicals and the sections on individual dye plants indicate which colours can be achieved when dyes are applied in this way.

The manufactured chemical mordant used most frequently by dyers is alum (aluminium sulphate or potassium aluminium sulphate), which is non-toxic, although it is an irritant and should not be ingested. For certain colours, iron or copper may also occasionally be used as mordants. However, as copper is poisonous I avoid using it if possible and no recipes in this book require a copper mordant. Other mordants or fixatives sometimes used are natural plant tannins and rhubarb leaf solution, which contains oxalic acid and is poisonous. Aluminium can also be extracted from clubmosses but in many areas, including parts of Britain, clubmosses are too rare for their use in dyeing to be environmentally acceptable, so clubmosses should only be harvested if they are abundant in your area.

NB: Before mordanting or dyeing, all fibres must be wetted out to ensure even penetration of whatever is being applied. The addition of a tiny amount of dishwashing liquid to the wetting-out water will aid this.

Mordanting with Alum

Alum mordant for animal fibres
10% aluminium sulphate (or potassium aluminium sulphate) or 2 teaspoons per 100g (4oz) of fibres

Dissolve the alum in boiling water, stirring well to ensure it has dissolved completely. Then add this to cool water in the pot and stir well again. Then add the wetted fibres, plus more water if necessary to ensure the fibres can move freely in the liquid. Put a lid on the pot, bring slowly to simmering point and hold at this temperature for an hour, moving the fibres around very gently from time to time. Leave the fibres to cool in the solution, overnight if possible, then remove them and rinse well.

This mordant can also be applied without heat. Add the dissolved alum to cool water, stir well then add the wetted fibres and leave them to soak for at least 24 hours, moving them around gently from time to time. Then remove them and rinse well.

The alum solution can be stored and re-used as the base for the next batch of fibres to be mordanted. I usually store the used alum mordant solution in a stainless steel or plastic bucket with a well-fitting lid. The second time I use it, I add the same quantities of alum as before (10%) but I add only about half the alum (5%) the third time. The next time I start adding 10% again, followed by 10%, then 5% and so on.

Making a mordant solution from aluminium sulphate

For this method the metric system must be used to ensure accuracy.
Aluminium sulphate (or potassium aluminium sulphate) in powder or granular form can be made into a mordant solution as follows:

Weigh up 100g of alum, put this into a heatproof measuring jug and add ¾ litre of boiling water. Stir very well to ensure the alum has dissolved completely then top up with hot water to the 1 litre/1000ml mark. Stir well again and leave to cool. This solution can be stored indefinitely in glass or strong plastic bottles. To use the solution, stir or shake it then measure off 10ml of solution for each 1g of mordant required. For example, for 5g of mordant you would use 50ml of mordant solution, for 10g you would use 100ml and so on. This is a particularly convenient system when mordanting with alum at 10% weight of fibres because you would use the same amount of mordant solution in millilitres as weight of fibre in grams. For example, for 450g of fibre you would use 450ml of alum solution.

Sometimes the alum can develop into lumps at the bottom of the container. If this happens, pour the entire contents, the lumps of alum included, into a pot and bring to simmering point. The alum should then re-dissolve and, when cool, it can be returned to the container.

Alum mordant for vegetable fibres

5% aluminium acetate or 2½ teaspoons per 100g (4oz) of fibres

Dissolve the alum acetate in boiling water, stirring well to make sure the fine powder has completely dissolved. Then add this to cool water in the pot and stir well again. Then add the wetted fibres, plus more water if necessary to enable them to move freely in the liquid. Put a lid on the pot, bring slowly to simmering point and hold at this temperature for an hour, moving the fibres around gently from time to time. Leave the fibres to cool in the solution, overnight if possible, then remove them and rinse. This alum acetate mordant can also be used on silk.

Mordanting with iron
For all fibres use 2% of ferrous (iron) sulphate or a ½ teaspoon per 100g (4oz) fibres

NB: Iron is harmful if ingested. Handle it carefully and wear rubber gloves.

Dissolve the iron sulphate in boiling water, stir well and then add this to cool water in the pot and stir well again. Then add the wetted fibres, plus more water if necessary to ensure they can move freely in the liquid. Put a lid on the pot, bring slowly to simmering point and then hold at this temperature for 30 minutes, moving the fibres around frequently to ensure even penetration. Allow the solution to cool a little then remove the fibres, squeeze any excess liquid back into the pot and rinse the fibres well several times. The remaining solution can be stored and then used as an iron modifier or re-used as the base for further mordant solutions.

Iron water can also be used as a mordant (see page 36 for details of how to make iron water). When used as a mordant, dilute the iron water at the rate of one part iron water solution to one part water and then use it as described above. Copper mordant can be made from copper sulphate or copper water in the same way as described above for iron mordant. However, as copper is poisonous, I avoid using it if possible.

Mordanting with tannin from plants
Tannin mordant for all fibres
25% (25g [1oz] per 100g [4oz] fibres) of crushed oak galls or 100% (100g [4oz] per 100g [4oz] fibres) chopped bramble leaves and tops (*Rubus fruticosus*) or 50% (50g [2oz] per 100g [4oz] fibres) chopped birch bark (*Betula spp.*), oak bark (*Quercus spp.*) or willow bark (*Salix spp.*)

Simmer the oak galls or bramble tops in water for 45 minutes, leave to cool then strain off the solution. Soak the birch, oak or willow bark in water for 24 hours then simmer it in the soaking water for 45 minutes to an hour and strain as above. Vegetable fibres and silk should be soaked in the cool tannin solution for 8–24 hours, moving them around from time to time. Wool fibres should be gently simmered in the solution for 20–30 minutes. Allow the fibres to cool in the mordant bath then remove them, squeeze well and rinse them.

Willow bark and birch bark usually give a pale pink colour to the fibres, so they are particularly useful as a base for red, coral and pink dyes. Bramble leaves and tops, oak bark and oak galls give a yellow-tan colour to the fibres, so they are useful as a base for yellow and brown dyes.

Mordanting with rhubarb leaves

In more remote areas in the Himalayas, where manufactured chemical mordants may be difficult to obtain, a solution made from rhubarb leaves is sometimes used as an alternative mordant for animal fibres. Rhubarb leaves contain oxalic acid, which is poisonous, so wear rubber gloves and handle rhubarb leaf solution with care. Rhubarb leaves give a pale yellow colour to the fibres and they can also be used as a dye. It is generally considered acceptable to add used rhubarb leaves or rhubarb leaf solution to the compost heap.

Rhubarb leaf mordant for animal fibres

100% chopped rhubarb leaves (*Rheum spp.*) fresh or dried (or 100g [4oz] per 100g [4oz] fibres)

Simmer the rhubarb leaves for an hour in plenty of water in a covered pot. Let the solution cool then strain it very carefully into a pot, avoiding splashes. Add the wetted fibres, plus more water if necessary to enable them to move freely in the liquid. Put a lid on the pot, then heat gradually to simmering point and simmer gently for 30–45 minutes. Leave the fibres to cool in the solution, then remove them and rinse well.

Mordanting with aluminium from clubmoss

Clubmosses are aluminium accumulators and have been used in the past as a source of aluminium mordant, especially in Scandinavia. Remains of a species of clubmoss unknown in Britain at that time were found at the ninth to eleventh century Viking-age site in York and suggest that the clubmoss was possibly brought to England by the Vikings for use as a mordant. Clubmosses are rare in many parts of the world and should only be harvested for mordanting purposes in areas where they are abundant.

The process of extracting and applying a clubmoss mordant takes several days to complete and is probably mainly of interest to students of historical dyeing techniques.

Clubmoss mordant for wool

200% finely chopped clubmoss (*Lycopodium spp.*) fresh or dried, or 200g (8oz) per 100g (4oz) fibres

Put the clubmoss into a dye pot, fill up with water and heat the mixture to 40 C/100 F. Keep it at this temperature for three days, then boil up the mixture once briefly, strain off the liquid and leave it to cool. Add the wool, plus more water if necessary, and heat slowly to 40 C/100 F. Turn off the heat. Repeat this heating process daily for three days. Allow the wool to cool in the solution, preferably overnight, then remove it, squeeze well and rinse briefly. The clubmoss solution can usually be re-used once more.

Extracting Dye Colour

Colour is extracted from most dyes by simmering the dyestuff for 45 minutes to an hour then straining off the liquid, which becomes the dye solution. With some dyes it may be possible to repeat this process once or even twice more to extract colour for further dye baths, which will produce successively paler shades. Some dyers add all the colour extractions together to make a single dye bath but this is really only necessary if the first extraction process doesn't provide enough colour for a dye bath.

To save heat, it is also possible to pour boiling or very hot water over the dyestuff and leave it to steep for several hours. This sometimes produces enough colour for a dye bath without the need for further heating. The dyestuff can then be steeped again or simmered for a second dye bath or dried and stored for re-use at a later date.

In my experience, most leaves and many tree barks need prolonged periods of gentle simmering to extract the dye colour and some dyestuffs, especially barks, benefit from prolonged soaking in cool water before heat is applied to extract more colour.

For dyers who wish to avoid the use of heat altogether, the fibres can be soaked without heat together with the dyestuff for as long as necessary to achieve a satisfactory depth of colour. Although this may not always give colours that are as deep or as vivid as those achieved from the application of heat, this method is useful with many dyes and saves energy.

Dyes and fibres soaking outside

Walnut hulls simmering gently

Alkaline extraction method

With some dyes, for example buckthorn bark, madder, rhubarb root and weld, colour extraction and application in an alkaline solution gives good results. For this method, the dyestuff is soaked for several days in the solution and no heat is required. For the alkaline solution, I usually use either two to three parts wood ash water (see page 35) to one part water or 2–3 teaspoons of washing soda or soda ash per 500ml/1 pint of water; the quantities do not need to be too precise and the pH value should be around pH10–11. Although the solution is alkaline initially, it becomes gradually neutral or slightly acidic as fermentation sets in. It is important to check the pH level daily, as once the solution loses its alkalinity the colour may change. For example, with madder, an alkaline solution can give shades of pink, which become coral or orange as fermentation sets in. If necessary, more wood ash water, washing soda or soda ash can be added to maintain alkalinity.

There are several ways of using this dye solution. In the first method, the fibres can be added to the solution together with the dyestuff at the outset and allowed to steep as described above. If you do this, finely chopped dyestuffs should be tied into a fine-meshed net or bag and the fibres should be moved around regularly in the liquid to ensure even dyeing. By adding fibres at different stages, several shades can be obtained. In the second method, the dye liquid is strained off after the dyestuff has been soaked in the alkaline solution for a few days, the fibres are added and soaked in this dye liquid for several days with no application of heat. Another method is to allow the dyestuff to soak for a few days as described above and then to simmer the dyestuff for about 30 minutes in the solution. The solution is then strained off, cooled a little and the fibres are added and left to soak for at least 24 hours with no application of heat.

NB: Remember not to heat alkaline solutions once the fibres have been added, especially if you are treating animal fibres such as wool, as a high level of alkalinity can severely damage some fibres if heat is applied.

One-step colour extraction and application
In order to save water and heat, colour can be extracted and applied in one process. This is successful with many plant dyes. Just put the dyestuff into the dye pot together with the wetted-out fibres, add hot or cold water then heat the dye bath and continue as described in the following section on applying dyes. With this method, it is advisable to tie finely chopped dyestuffs into a fine-meshed net or bag first and the fibres should be moved around regularly in the liquid to ensure even dyeing.

Application of Dyes

Once the colour has been extracted from the dyestuff and the dye solution has been strained off, the dye bath is ready for use. If the dye bath is still hot, allow it to cool before adding the fibres, as sudden changes of temperature may cause wool and some other animal fibres to felt. Make sure the fibres have been wetted out then add them to the dye bath, plus more water if necessary to ensure they can move freely in the solution. Then gently heat the dye bath to simmering point and simmer for about 45 minutes. Turn off the heat and leave the fibres to cool in the dye bath, overnight if possible, before rinsing them well and then washing them. With some dyes, I heat the dye bath, plus the fibres, to simmering point and then remove it from the heat and allow the fibres to soak in the dye bath for as long as necessary to achieve the required depth of colour.

Some dyes can be successfully applied without any heat at all. Just strain off the dye solution, add the fibres and leave them to soak in the dye bath for as long as necessary to achieve the desired depth of colour.

If there is enough colour potential remaining in the used dye bath, it can be re-used for paler shades. This is known as an "exhaust" dye bath. Some dyes, for example madder, seem inexhaustible and I have often used a madder dye bath three, four and even five times, obtaining successively paler shades.

A small number of dyes are not applied in the ways described above and for these dyes special instructions are given in the sections on individual plants.

Washing naturally dyed fibres

When washing naturally dyed materials it is important to use a washing medium with a neutral pH, otherwise unwanted colour changes may occur. I usually wash dyed fibres in a solution of hand-hot water and dishwashing liquid, using about a ½ teaspoon of dishwashing liquid per 7 litres (1½ gallons) of water. I have tested most common brands of dish-washing liquid and all were pH neutral when in solution. I avoid using soap flakes, as soap tends to be alkaline. Whatever washing medium you select, it is wise to test it on a small dyed sample before using it for larger batches of fibres. The same applies if you think you may need to wash dyed materials at higher temperatures or in a washing machine. The sections on Cleaning Fibres for Dyeing (page 22) and Testing for Fastness (page 38) give further information.

Colour Modifiers

The range of shades from each dye you use can be increased by modifying the colours on the fibres after they have been dyed.

The simplest modifiers are those which act by altering the pH value of the solution. This means that if you add an acid or an alkali to water or to the used dye bath and then treat the dyed fibres in this liquid, you will usually alter the colour of the fibres. The colour change may be quite dramatic or only very slight, depending on the degree of pH sensitivity of the dye used and also on how much acid or alkali was added to the solution and how long the fibres were left in it.

In addition, iron and copper solutions can be used as modifiers instead of mordants. They will not only modify the colours but usually also improve their fastness. For those who like to be self-sufficient wherever possible, iron and copper solutions, or waters, can be made using scrap iron or lengths of copper piping (details on page 36). Some dyers use pots made of iron or copper instead but, at least in my experience, this does not tend to have the same effect as using iron or copper solutions as modifiers. With many dyes, iron and copper modifiers give very similar colours and as copper is poisonous some dyers may prefer to avoid using it.

An alkaline modifier made from wood ash water or washing soda is, in my view, the most useful of the colour modifiers. Many dye colours which are applied without alum as a pre-mordant will become brighter and clearer if an alkaline modifier is used after dyeing. Weld, for example, if used without an alum mordant but with an alkaline modifier, will give colours almost as bright as those from an alum mordant.

Acidic modifiers, such as clear vinegar, citric acid and lemon or lime juice, are less useful than the other modifiers and do not tend to produce significant colour changes with many dyes. They can be used with red dyes, such as madder, to shift the colour towards orange and will make mustard shades yellower in tone. When testing a dye for the first time, it is a good idea to try out all the modifiers but in my experience acidic modifiers do not have a significant effect on the colours from many natural dyes.

It is also possible to use multiple modifiers. For example: fibres modified in an alkaline solution can then be modified in an iron or copper solution. This is very useful if an alum mordant is not used. The alkaline modifier will deepen the dyed colour and the iron or copper modifiers will usually increase its fastness.

How to make modifier solutions

The quantities given below are suggestions for initial experiments. Modifier solutions can vary in concentration and the colour changes achieved will depend on the strength of the modifier solution, the quantity that is added and the length of time that the fibres are soaked in the modifier solution. Any remaining modifier solutions can be stored indefinitely in clearly labelled strong plastic or glass bottles.

Acidic modifiers

To make an acidic modifier solution, dissolve 4–5 teaspoons of citric acid granules in 500ml (1 pint) of boiling water or use clear vinegar (5% acetic acid) or lemon or lime juice.

Alkaline modifiers

To make an alkaline modifier solution, dissolve 4–5 teaspoons of washing soda or soda ash in 500ml (1 pint) of boiling water or use wood ash water.

Wood ash water

Wood ash water is easy to make, especially if you have a wood-burning stove. Just remove the cold wood ashes, put them in a large container with a lid (a strong plastic bucket is fine) and fill up with water. Leave the ashes to soak for a week or two, by which time the solution should be yellowish in colour and will feel slick or slimy to the touch. Then pour or siphon off the liquid without disturbing the ash sediment and use this liquid as your modifier. Any remaining solution can be stored indefinitely.

Wood ash water can also be used for the alkaline colour extraction method (see page 32 for details).

Iron and copper modifiers

To make iron and copper modifier solutions, dissolve 3–4 teaspoons of ferrous (iron) sulphate or copper sulphate in 500ml (1 pint) of boiling water. Or use iron or copper waters instead.

NB: Handle iron and copper sulphates with care as copper is poisonous and iron is harmful if ingested.

Iron and copper waters

Instead of using iron sulphate and copper sulphate, it is possible to make iron and copper solutions, or waters, by dissolving the metals in water and clear vinegar (5% acetic acid), as described in the following sections. These solutions can be used as mordants or as colour modifiers. The solutions are used without dilution as colour modifiers but if used as mordants they should be diluted at the rate of one part solution to one part water.

Iron water

Put some rusty nails or pieces of scrap iron into a large lidded glass jar or a strong plastic container with a lid. Make a solution of two parts water to one part clear vinegar and add this to the iron pieces in the container. Put the lid on firmly and leave the mixture to steep for a week or two until the solution is rust coloured. To use the solution, strain off the required amount. The solution can be topped up with more water/vinegar solution as required.

Copper water

Proceed as above for iron water but using lengths of copper piping instead of scrap iron and equal parts of water and clear vinegar. After a few weeks, when the solution has become blue, it is ready for use. Use as described for iron water.

Using the modifier solutions

• These can be either added to the used dye bath, to which the dyed materials are returned and then soaked or simmered, or added to a separate pot of water, in which the dyed materials are then treated.
• All the modifiers can be applied without heat, although heat can be used with acidic, iron and copper modifiers, if necessary, to speed up the process.
• Do not heat alkaline modifier solutions, especially if treating wool which may disintegrate in hot alkaline solutions.
• Start by adding a small amount of the modifier solution. If after 30 minutes the colour change is not significant, add a little more. Keep on adding more until you are satisfied with the results.
• Keep separate stirring spoons for each modifier so the solutions cannot contaminate each other. This is particularly important with iron modifiers, as iron can severely contaminate other solutions and make them useless.
• Do not use the same modifier solution for more than one dye unless the dyes produce similar colours. For example, it is fine to use the same modifier solutions for weld and dyer's broom, as they give similar colours, but it would not be advisable to use this same solution for madder.

Using multiple modifiers

If you use more than one modifier on the same fibres, remember to rinse the fibres well after applying the first modifier and before using the next modifier. Otherwise, any residues from the first modifier may contaminate the second modifier solution.

Re-using modifier solutions

In order to avoid discarding solutions unnecessarily, I sometimes return the used modifier solutions to their containers and label them according to the dyes with which they have been used. So I have one iron modifier container labelled "For use with weld and dyer's broom" and another labelled "For use with madder". After a while the solutions begin to look murky and become discoloured and should be discarded. Iron solutions can be poured on the garden around broad-leaved evergreens, otherwise discard the solutions on the ground in an isolated spot away from septic tanks or where children or pets may play. The quantities remaining should be so small that they are unlikely to cause problems.

Workshop samples showing some of the effects of modifiers on fibres dyed with weld (top row left), rhubarb root (second row left), buckthorn bark (top row right) and madder (second row right)

Testing for Fastness

It is important to test dyed materials for light-fastness and wash-fastness, especially if you are producing items for sale.

Light-fastness testing
Sandwich the dyed samples between sheets of card, leaving a portion of the dyed sample uncovered. Then place the samples in a window which doesn't face directly into full sunlight and leave them for a month or two. Check from time to time to see how much they have faded. You can use a sample of alum-mordanted wool dyed in madder as a "control", as this has good fastness properties. If the samples fade at a similar rate to the "control", they will have similar light-fastness properties. If they fade more rapidly they will be less suitable for projects where good light-fastness is crucial.

Wash-fastness testing
Testing for wash-fastness is a little more laborious. You need to find out not only whether a dye washes out, but also whether it will stain other materials. It is also important to subject the samples to the same type of wash you are likely to use for any finished projects. Some samples may need to be put through the appropriate washing machine programme, others will require only a brief hand-wash. If you are not sure what you are likely to use the dyed materials for, wash one sample by hand and one in the washing machine. This means three samples of each dyed fibre are needed: one to remain unwashed for comparison purposes, one for the washing machine and one for the hand-wash.

If you are testing dyed fabrics, you will need some small pieces of undyed woollen and cotton fabrics. Sandwich the dyed sample between a layer of undyed cotton fabric and a layer of undyed woollen fabric. Sew around the edges to join all three pieces together. Make a second "sandwich" in the same way, then wash one in the washing machine and wash the other by hand. Then open up each "sandwich" and check first of all whether the samples have stained the other fabrics. Some dyes may stain both the cotton and the wool, while others may stain only one of the fabrics. Then compare the samples with the third, unwashed, sample to see how much of the colour has been washed out in each of the washing processes. If you have dyed yarns rather than pieces of fabric, make two tight plaits, each consisting of two or three strands of the dyed yarn, plus two or three strands of an undyed woollen yarn and two or three strands of an undyed cotton yarn. Make sure each plait is firmly secured at both ends, then wash as for the "sandwiches". Keep an unwashed sample of the dyed yarn for comparison purposes.

Some examples of natural dyes on silk

From left: indigo (4 samples) lichen purple (4 samples), all NM

*From left: yellow dock root+A, yellow dock root, rhubarb root, weld+A,
rhubarb root & woad, dyer's broom+A, onion skins+A, buckthorn bark,
willow bark, walnut hulls, all NM & cold soak only*

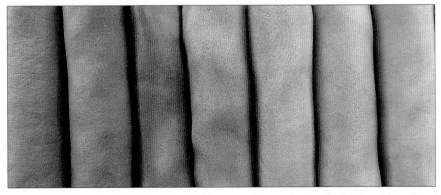

From left: oak bark+I (2 samples), madder root (5 samples), all NM & cold soak only

Other Techniques

Contact Dyeing on Fabric using Plant Materials

One of the earliest methods of colouring and patterning fabric was probably by means of basic contact dyeing. I imagine that early peoples would have experimented by squeezing the juice from berries directly onto fibres or cloth and one progression from squeezing juice on to cloth is to use plant materials in direct contact with fabric to make patterns.

For dyers who wish to dye fabrics and would also prefer to use little or no water or heat, this is a useful alternative method of applying colour to create designs on cloth.

Selecting plant materials
For this technique you need fresh plant materials such as leaves, flowers, bark and berries. Most leaves with a clearly defined shape and strong colour are suitable, especially leaves from ornamental trees. Leaves which have developed their rich autumn colours also work well, as do fallen leaves or leaves which have fallen to the ground and become dry. The most successful fresh flower heads and petals are those which have a rich colour, such as purple pansies and petunias and red, purple, orange and yellow dahlias. Dried chopped dyestuffs, such as madder root, buckthorn bark and rhubarb root, can also be used and onion skins are particularly effective. Used tea or coffee grounds can be sprinkled on too.

Adding other items for extra interest
Metallic objects, such as rusty nails, paper clips, copper coins, curtain rings and old keys can be used to add extra interest to the designs. These objects react with the dyes and make impressions on the cloth, especially if they are sprayed with vinegar before the cloth is folded.

This method of creating patterns on fabric offers great scope for experimenting and it is always worth trying whatever plant materials or metallic objects you have available, as sometimes the least promising materials can produce pleasing results.

Selecting fabrics
This technique can be used successfully on silk, cotton, linen and fine wool fabrics, which should first be washed thoroughly. I prefer to mordant the fabric, either with alum or plant tannins, but unmordanted materials can also be used, especially if metal objects are added, although the colours achieved may be paler. The fabric should be dampened before use.

Method

Spread out the damp fabric on a flat surface (with plastic beneath to protect the surface if necessary), arrange the plant material to make a pattern on the surface of one half of the fabric and spray well with water. For extra detail, add some small metal objects, such as rusty nails, curtain rings, old keys, paper clips etc. Used tea leaves and coffee grounds can also be sprinkled over the surface.

Spray with clear vinegar, particularly over the metal objects, and fold the fabric over so the plant materials etc. are covered by the second half of the fabric.

Then carefully fold the fabric into a tight bundle. Tie the bundle with string, cover it with clingfilm or plastic wrap and then leave it to mature for several weeks, preferably in a warm place such as an airing cupboard or in a warm compost bin. Alternatively, the fabric bundle can be steamed for 45 minutes to set the colour. For this, I use a vegetable steamer reserved for this purpose only. When the fabric bundle is unwrapped, there should be clear prints of the plant materials used, with darker details where the metal has made imprints.

Details of contact prints on silk fabric (above) and cotton fabric (below)

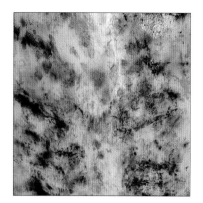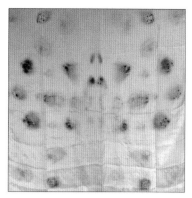

Left: Detail of contact print on silk using onion skins, petunias and rusty nails
Right: Contact print on silk using pansy, geranium and dyer's chamomile flowers

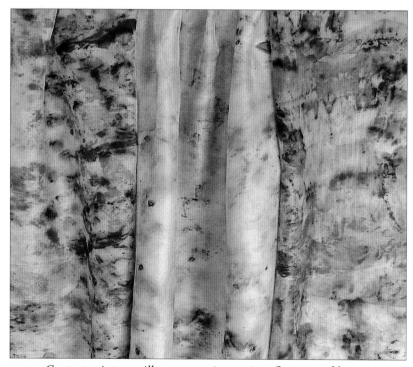

Contact prints on silk scarves using various flowers and leaves,
onion skins, coffee grounds, paper clips and rusty nails

Thanks to India Flint, who originally discovered the eucalyptus eco-print and also developed the printing technique used above and the following technique for dyeing with frozen flowers (page 43). Full details are in her books *Eco Colour* and *Second Skin* (see Bibliography).

Dyeing with Frozen Flowers

This technique requires no heat and is a good way of using faded or dead flower heads, especially some of those not usually considered useful for dyeing. The flowers must be frozen before use. It seems to work best with flowers rich in anthocyanins, so whenever I dead-head plants with deep red or purple flowers, such as pansies or petunias, I put the flower heads into a plastic bag and store them in the freezer. When the bag is full, or when I have two or three handfuls of frozen flowers, I make a dye bath.

To make the dye bath, tie the frozen flowers into a fine-meshed net or bag or piece of similar fine fabric and then put them into a bowl or pot of cool water and squeeze well to extract the colour. Continue squeezing until no further colour seems to be coming from the flowers, then remove the bag and discard the flowers. If I am dyeing unmordanted materials, at this point I usually add a teaspoon or two of alum sulphate to the dye solution to improve the colour fastness. Stir well then add the materials to be dyed, plus more water if necessary to enable them to move freely in the liquid, and leave them to soak in the cool dye solution for several hours or overnight. I have found that this method tends to produce soft green-blue shades and I have successfully dyed wool, silk and cotton this way.

Frozen pansies

Colours on silk (NM)

Colours on cotton (NM)

From top: cotton, wool (NM)

Over-dyeing and Multi-coloured Skeins and Fabrics

Compound colours are achieved by dyeing one colour over another. The usual colour principles apply, so a yellow dye and a red dye will produce orange and a yellow dye and a blue dye will give green and so on. Although green is the most common colour in nature, a true grass green cannot be achieved from a single dye and is made by dyeing yellow over blue or vice-versa. It doesn't usually make any difference which of the colours one starts with and the depth and tone of colour can be adjusted according to the strength of the dye baths and the length of time the fibres are immersed in each one. Sometimes several dyes are required to produce a particular colour. For example, black is created by applying red, yellow and blue dyes in sequence.

Wool skeins showing shades of turquoise and green from weld (yellow) overdyed in woad (blue)

Top: madder (NM) and below: madder, overdyed in blue from woad (wool skeins on silk fabric)

Black from madder + weld + woad

Multi-coloured skeins and fabrics

There are several ways of producing variegated or multi-coloured skeins of yarn and lengths of fabric. The simplest method is probably to use colour modifiers, although this can sometimes produce variations on a single colour, rather than several different colours, depending on the dyestuff used. Colour variations can also be achieved by using more than one mordant or dye on a single skein or length of fabric.

For the techniques described below, the skeins or fabric lengths need to be fairly long and must be arranged so that just the right amount of fibre or fabric is entered into the solution each time. It is also important to ensure that no sections of the skeins or fabric lengths are allowed to hang over the sides of the pots, as this will cause the liquid to "creep" along the fibres and seep on to the floor or work surface.

I usually suspend the skein or fabric length over a pole, the height of which can be adjusted according to the length of the skein or fabric and depending on how much of it is to be dyed in each dye. The skein or fabric can be rotated around the pole as necessary. Another method would be to wrap the skein or fabric around the pole, leaving the sections to be immersed in the dye pots unwrapped. A pole which has one flat edge is useful and less likely to roll off the top of the dye pots.

Two different ways of suspending a skein over dye pots

Colour variations from colour modifiers

For variations using colour modifiers, dye the skein or piece of fabric using your chosen dyestuff then prepare the modifier solutions. Place one end of the skein or fabric in the first modifier solution and the other end in the second modifier solution, leaving a central section unmodified. Leave the skein or fabric to steep in the solutions until each of the three sections is a different shade from the others.

Skein of wool (NM) dyed in onion skins, with an alkaline modifier applied to one end (left) and an iron modifier applied to the other end (right)

Colour variations from mordants

Variations in colour can be achieved by applying different mordants to each end of a skein or to different sections of a length of fabric. For this you need to make up two mordant solutions and then place one end of the skein or fabric in one mordant bath and the other end in the second mordant bath. A central section could remain unmordanted and this would produce a third shade.

Wool skein mordanted with iron on one end (left) and alum on the other end (right) then dyed in madder, followed by an alkaline modifier

Colour variations from several dyes

Method 1
Select two dyes and dye one end of the skein or length of fabric in the first dye and the other end in the second dye. If the two dyes are allowed to run into each other at the central section, a third colour can be achieved.

Skein dyed in indigo (blue) and walnut hulls (brown)
with a central area of overlap (grey-green)

Method 2
Bind several strong plastic or string ties over some sections of the skein or fabric length and then dye it in the first dye. Leave to cool then rinse well and squeeze out any excess liquid. Remove some of the ties, in order to reveal some undyed sections, and add more ties to cover some of the dyed areas. Prepare the second dye bath and dye the skein, or fabric length, again. Leave to cool then rinse well and remove all of the ties. Rinse again and wash. This method results in a space-dyed skein or fabric length with three different shades: dye colour one, dye colour two and a third colour from colour one over-dyed by colour two as well as some undyed sections.

Method 3
Wrap the skein, or fabric length, around pieces of iron and/or lengths of copper piping and bind it round tightly in several places. Then dye the skein in the first dye bath. Allow the skein to cool then untie it and unwrap it from the metal pieces. Bind some ties around the skein to cover some of the dyed areas, wrap the skein around the metal pieces again and bind it round in several places as before. Then dye the skein in the second dye bath. Leave the skein in the dye bath to cool, then remove it but allow it to "rest" for several hours or overnight before removing the metal pieces. Then rinse the skein well and wash it.

The Dye Plants

Introduction
Wherever one lives, there will be plants that can be used for dyeing and one of the pleasures is experimenting with native or local plants. One aim of my most recent dye experiments was to try out some of the native plants that are common in my area.
As so many plants give colours in the tan to yellow and brown range, dyers should be able to select plants local to them for these colours. Relatively few plants are sources of blues, reds, corals and pinks, so any plants capable of producing these colours should be valued and perhaps grown as garden plants if necessary. For those dyers unable to gather or grow their own dye plants, most of the dyestuffs mentioned below can be purchased as dried plant materials from specialist dyestuff suppliers or from suppliers of culinary and medicinal herbs.
   If you gather your own plant dyestuffs from the wild or from the garden, remember that leaves will often give different shades, depending on the time of year at which they are harvested.
Also, the colours from leaves and flowers may vary according to whether they are used fresh or dried. Commercially produced plant dyestuffs usually give more consistent colours because they tend to be processed under more controlled conditions and growers are likely to regularly harvest them at the same time of year.
Most of the dye plants featured in this section are native to Britain and the majority of these will also be available in other parts of the world, although the individual species may differ. For example, the native British oaks are *Quercus robur* and *Quercus petraea* but other species of *Quercus* occur elsewhere and all species can be used in the same way in the dye pot.

All plants not native to Britain are indicated with an asterisk on the plant pages. For example: *Eucalyptus spp.* Eucalyptus *

Abbreviations used for the dyed samples
Br. = brown wool, Gr. = grey wool, NM = no mordant,
AM = alum mordant, tannin(W) = tannin mordant from willow bark,
tannin(B) = tannin mordant from bramble tops, RL = rhubarb leaf mordant, CL = clubmoss mordant, +A = alkaline modifier used,
+C = copper modifier used, +I = iron modifier used, +A+I = alkaline and iron modifiers used. All samples are wool unless otherwise indicated.

Basic dyeing methods for all plants unless otherwise stated

Dyeing with heat
Simmer the dyestuff for 45 minutes to extract the colour then strain off the dye liquid. Allow the dye liquid to cool a little, especially if dyeing wool fibres, then add the fibres, plus more water if necessary to ensure they can move freely. Heat gradually to simmering point and simmer for 45 minutes. Leave the fibres to cool in the dye bath, preferably overnight, then rinse well and wash. (Refer to the percentage system on page 26 to calculate dyestuff quantities.)

Dyeing without heat
If the dyestuff pieces are very small or likely to be difficult to remove from the fibres after dyeing, first tie them into a fine-meshed net or bag. Then put the dyestuff and the fibres into a strong container with a lid and add enough hot or cold water to allow the fibres to move freely. Put on the lid then leave the fibres to soak for as long as necessary to achieve a suitable colour. To ensure even dyeing, move the fibres around in the container from time to time. Finally remove the fibres, shake out any dyestuff pieces, rinse well and wash. If after a week or so the colour has not developed well enough, try dyeing with heat as described above. (Refer to the percentage system on page 26 to calculate dyestuff quantities.)

Using the alkaline extraction method
When this dyeing method is indicated in the individual plant entries refer to the instructions on page 32 and to calculate dyestuff quantities refer to the percentage system on page 26.

Tannin, used as a mordant or base for other colours, tends in general to make the dyed colours deeper, but not brighter, in tone. Where applicable, further comments on the effects of tannin mordants are made in the individual plant entries. If naturally pigmented grey and brown wool fibres are used, the colours obtained are often richer. The use of grey fibres can be particularly effective with yellow dyes, which often give attractive green shades when applied to grey fibres. If the colours produced on grey and brown fibres appear pale, an alkaline modifier can usually intensify and enhance them. Iron and copper modifiers often give very similar shades of mossy green. Where the colours from iron and copper modifiers differ significantly, this is indicated in the individual plant entries.

The dye plants in alphabetical order of Latin names

52 *Acer pseudoplatanus* Sycamore
53 *Achillea millefolium* Common
Yarrow
54 *Allium cepa* Onion
55 *Alnus spp.* Alder
56 *Anthemis tinctoria* Dyer's
Chamomile
58 *Arctostaphylos uva-ursi*
Bearberry
59 *Berberis spp.* Barberry
60 *Betula spp.* Birch
61 *Buddleia spp.* Buddleia
63 *Calluna vulgaris* Heather
64 *Centaurea nigra* Knapweed
65 *Chamaemelum nobile*
Chamomile
66 *Cornus sanguinea* Dogwood
67 *Dahlia spp.* Dahlia
69 *Epilobium spp.* Willow Herb
70 *Equisetum arvense* Horsetail
71 *Eucalyptus spp.* Eucalyptus
73 *Eupatorium cannabinum* Hemp
Agrimony
74 *Fagus spp.* Beech
75 *Frangula alnus* Alder Buckthorn
76 *Fraxinus spp.* Ash
77 *Galium mollugo* Hedge
Bedstraw
78 *Galium odoratum* Sweet
Woodruff

79 *Galium verum* Lady's Bedstraw
80 *Genista tinctoria* Dyer's Broom
82 *Hedera helix* Ivy
83 *Humulus lupulus* Common Hop
84 *Hypericum spp.* St. John's Wort
86 *Isatis tinctoria* Woad
102 *Juglans spp.* Walnut
104 *Juniperus communis* Juniper
105 *Malus spp.* Apple
106 *Prunus spp.* Cherry
107 *Quercus spp.* Oak
109 *Reseda luteola* Weld
111 *Rhamnus spp.* Buckthorn
114 *Rheum spp.* Rhubarb
116 *Rubia peregrina* Wild Madder
117 *Rubia tinctorum* Dyer's Madder
124 *Rubus fruticosus* Blackberry
125 *Rumex spp.* Dock, Sorrel
126 *Salix spp.* Willow
128 *Salvia officinalis* Sage
129 *Sambucus spp.* Elder
130 *Serratula tinctoria* Saw-wort
131 *Solidago spp.* Goldenrod
132 *Tanacetum parthenium*
Feverfew
133 *Tanacetum vulgare* Tansy
134 *Taxus baccata* Yew
135 *Tilia cordata* Lime

A country lane with many useful sources of dye colour

Acer pseudoplatanus Sycamore *

Sycamore leaves

Acer pseudoplatanus, also called the sycamore maple, is not generally considered to be native to Britain, although there is a suggestion that it may have been present here since the Bronze Age and that pollen from burials of that period which have been identified as being from field maple may actually have been from sycamore. It has become naturalised here and is often planted in cities because of its tolerance of urban pollution. Sycamore has winged seeds which catch the wind and then fall to the ground, causing seedlings to spring up everywhere. These seeds can also be used in the dye pot and give similar colours to those from the leaves. Without an alum mordant, sycamore leaves give a warm tan colour, which is deepened and brightened by an alkaline modifier. An alkaline modifier followed by an iron modifier gives a rich moss green and a copper modifier gives a lime green. Use 150% to 200% dyestuff.

Colours from sycamore leaves
Left: Br.NM, Gr.NM; Centre from top: AM, NM, NM+A, NM+C, NM+A+I;
Right: tannin(W), tannin(B)

Achillea millefolium Common Yarrow

Common yarrow

Achillea millefolium is a common perennial plant that grows wild on roadsides and in woodlands and fields. It has grey-green feathery leaves and flat pink or white flower heads. There are many hybrid species of *Achillea* and all can be used in the dye pot. Yarrow can be bought as plants or grown from seed and plants from seeds sown indoors in early spring will often flower in their first summer. Once established, yarrow plants usually spread of their own accord. The whole plant top is used for dyeing and can be used fresh or dried for later use. When harvesting yarrow, cut off the leaves and whole flowering tops close to the base, as this will encourage new growth. Yarrow gives lemon yellow shades with an alum mordant. If used without an alum mordant, yarrow gives pale tan colours; an alkaline modifier deepens the colour a little and copper and iron modifiers give soft green shades. Use 200% dyestuff.

Colours from yarrow plant tops
Left: Br.NM+A, Gr.NM+A; Centre from top: AM, NM, NM+A, NM+C,
NM+I, NM+A+I; Right: tannin(W)+A, tannin(B)

Allium cepa Onion *

Onion skins

Although the common onion is not a native British plant and probably originated from Central Asia, it was widely cultivated in Britain from an early date. It does not appear to have been a traditional dye source in the more distant past but it has been popular among craft dyers for many years. It features here not only because of the lovely colours onion skins give but also because they were among the very first dyes I used as a novice dyer. Whenever you peel an onion, put the skins in a paper bag and save them until you have enough for a dye bath. The outer skins of the brown culinary onion give vibrant shades of rust, gold and yellow. Red onion skins are best used separately, as they often give different shades. Onion skins can be used successfully without an alum mordant and can give attractive colours on naturally pigmented grey and brown wool fibres. Use 100% dyestuff.

Colours from onion skins
Left: Br.NM; Centre from top: AM, NM, NM+A, NM+C, NM+I;
Right: tannin(B)

Alnus spp. Alder

Common alder leaves *Alder cones*

Common alder, *Alnus glutinosa*, is abundant throughout most of Europe. The leaves, twigs, bark and brown cones of all species of alder can be used in the dye pot without an alum mordant. The leaves give yellow-tan shades and the cones give useful browns when used with alkaline and iron modifiers. Alder cones, twigs and bark are rich in tannin and can be used as a tannin mordant. The bark gives grey shades with an iron modifier. For all parts of alder, use 150% to 200% dyestuff.

Above: colours from alder leaves
Left: Br.NM+A, Gr.NM+A; Centre from top: AM, NM, NM+A, NM+C, NM+I,
NM+A+I; Right: tannin(B), tannin(W)
Below: colours from alder cones (Samples as for alder leaves but no NM+A+I)

Anthemis tinctoria Dyer's Chamomile *

Dyer's chamomile

Dyer's chamomile is a short-lived perennial plant, native to the Mediterranean and Western Asia. It is a traditional source of dye in many parts of Europe and its flowers are used for some of the yellows in Turkish carpets and kilims. Dyer's chamomile has attractively cut leaves and yellow daisy-like flowers. Most other types of chamomile have white flowers and these are the ones usually found growing in the wild. *Anthemis nobilis*, now called *Chamaemelum nobile*, can also be used as a dyestuff (see page 65).

Dyer's chamomile is easy to grow from seed and makes a very attractive garden plant. Sow the seeds indoors several weeks before the last frosts, as plants started early enough will flower in their first summer. Transplant the seedlings to their permanent sites as soon as they are strong enough and keep them well watered. Dyer's chamomile is generally trouble-free and will adapt to most soil conditions. The leaves can be harvested at any time during the growing season. Pick the flower heads as they pass their prime and use them fresh or dry them ready for use when you have collected enough for a dye bath. Keep the leaves and stalks separate from the flowers, as they give slightly different shades in the dye pot. If dyer's chamomile flowers are used alone to make a dye bath, they give clear bright yellows when used with an alum mordant. Without an alum mordant, the flowers used alone give shades of pale yellow; an alkaline modifier intensifies the colour, and iron and copper modifiers give mossy greens. A tannin mordant gives a deeper mustard tone. The leaves and stalks of dyer's chamomile give delicate shades of pale yellow, tan and green. When used with an alum mordant they give soft greenish yellows; if used without an alum mordant the colours are paler. A tannin mordant deepens the colours, copper and iron modifiers give soft greens and an alkaline modifier gives an attractive deeper moss green. Rich moss green shades can be achieved on naturally pigmented grey and brown wool fibres if an alkaline modifier is used. Use 100% to 150% dyestuff for the flowers and 200% for the leaves and stalks.

Colours from dyer's chamomile flowers
Left: Br.NM+A, Gr.NM+A; Centre from top: AM, NM, NM+A,
NM+C, NM+I; Right: tannin(B), tannin(B)+A

Colours from dyer's chamomile leaves and stalks
Left: Br.NM+A, Gr.NM+A; Centre from top: AM, NM, NM+A,
NM+C, NM+I; Right: tannin(B), tannin(B)+A

Arctostaphylos uva-ursi Bearberry or Uva-ursi

Bearberry

Bearberry, or uva-ursi, is a small low-growing evergreen shrub which has adapted to Arctic and Sub-arctic climates. It prefers acidic soils and in Britain it is found mainly in the north. The leaves are used in herbal medicines and they can also be used in the dye pot. In Scandinavian countries bearberry leaves were used to produce grey and black dyes on wool. To make a dye bath from bearberry leaves, first soak the leaves overnight in hot water. Then simmer them for 45 minutes to an hour, strain off the dye liquid and simmer the fibres gently in the solution for another hour. Allow the fibres to cool in the dye bath, preferably overnight, before rinsing them. With an alum mordant bearberry leaves give a soft yellow; without an alum mordant the colour is paler. An iron modifier gives a rich grey colour but to achieve a deep grey-black colour, fibres should first be mordanted with iron, then dyed and treated in an iron modifier after dyeing. Use 150% to 200% dyestuff.

Colours from bearberry leaves
Left: Br.NM+A, Gr.NM+A; Centre from top: AM, NM, NM+A, NM+C, NM+I;
Right: tannin(B)

Berberis spp. Barberry

Berberis darwinii   *Chopped barberry bark*

Barberry can be found in most parts of Europe, although it is rare in the Mediterranean. The yellow dye from barberry bark is traditionally used in Europe, especially in Scandinavia. *Berberis vulgaris* is the native British species of barberry but in some parts of the world *Berberis vulgaris* is banned because it acts as a host for stem rust, which can cause damage to cereal and grain crops. However, other species of barberry, such as *Berberis darwinii* and *Berberis thunbergii*, can be used as alternatives. With an alum mordant barberry bark gives clear yellow colours. If used without an alum mordant barberry bark gives paler yellows, which can be deepened slightly with an alkaline modifier. Iron and copper modifiers give attractive shades of soft green. Use 150% dyestuff.

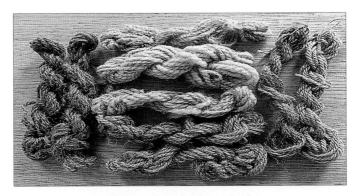

Colours from barberry bark
Left: Br.NM+A, Gr.NM+A; Centre from top: AM, NM, NM+A, NM+C,
NM+I; Right: tannin(W), tannin(B)

Betula spp. Birch

Birch leaves   *Birch bark*

Birches are ancient trees and in many parts of the world various species have been used as dye sources for centuries. The bark and leaves of birch can be used without an alum mordant, although the yellow obtained from the leaves is pale unless an alkaline modifier is used. With iron and copper modifiers the leaves give soft greens. Birch bark needs to be simmered for at least an hour to extract the colour; it gives soft pink/tan shades and a deeper pink if an alum mordant is used. Use at least 150% dyestuff for both leaves and bark.

Colours from birch leaves (above) and birch bark (below)
Left: Br.NM, Gr.NM; Centre from top: AM, CL (no CL below), NM, NM+A, NM+C,
NM+I; Right: tannin(W), tannin(B) (also tannin(B)+A below)

Buddleia spp. Buddleia *

Pink-flowering Buddleia davidii   *Buddleia x weyeriana*

There are many species of buddleia, a perennial shrub native to some warmer regions of North and South America and some parts of Asia and Africa. Buddleia attracts butterflies, so for that reason alone it is a welcome addition to the garden. The species most commonly grown in gardens is *Buddleia davidii*, native to China. Buddleia is also a great coloniser of dry open ground and it often self-sows on waste ground and can frequently be found growing wild. Buddleia is a very useful dye plant and can be used successfully without a mordant. The part of the plant that gives the most colour in the dye pot is the dead flower head, so every time you dead-head the plant save the flower heads for dyeing. It doesn't appear to matter what colour the flowers are, as they all seem to produce similar dye colours, so I mix the dead flower heads from my yellow, pink and purple buddleia bushes. (However, I have never tried the dead-heads from white buddleia, which may be less effective in the dye pot.) I usually collect the dead-heads and spread them out in a dark place on newspaper until I have enough to make a dye bath. Any surplus flower heads can be dried and stored for later use. Buddleia leaves and stems can also be used to make a dye bath and give slightly paler shades than the dead flower heads. Buddleia gives yellow to mustard colours and deeper mustards on a tannin base. An alkaline modifier intensifies the colours, and iron and copper modifiers give soft greens. Buddleia can be used successfully without heating the dye bath if you start off by adding boiling water. Just put the plant pieces plus the fibres to be dyed into a heatproof container, cover with boiling water and put on the lid. Leave the fibres to soak until they have taken up enough colour and move them around occasionally. As the buddleia pieces can be difficult to remove from fibres, it may be advisable to tie them into a fine-meshed net or bag first, rather than leaving them loose in the dye pot. Use 100% to 150% dyestuff for both dead flower heads and leaves and stems.

Colours from dried dead buddleia flower heads
Left: Br.NM, Gr.NM;
Centre from top: NM (tiny silk skein), AM, NM, NM+A, NM+C, NM+I;
Right: tannin(W), tannin(B)

Left: colours from a "dead flower heads only" dye bath
Right: colours from a "leaves and stems only" dye bath
Each set from top: NM, AM, NM+I

Calluna vulgaris Heather

Heather flowering tops

Heather has long been valued as a source of dye in Scotland. Heathers make attractive perennial garden plants and grow best in peaty, acid soils, but should not be planted in pure peat. Some may tolerate chalky soils or those with a small amount of lime. They like an open, sunny position and require plenty of water. Heathers bought from nurseries are best planted out in spring and autumn and set deeply, so that the entire stem is buried. For dyeing, use either the whole flowering tops or just the flowers alone. Heather can be used without an alum mordant. The stems add tannin to the dye bath, so using the whole flowering tops tends to give muted green-gold and light brown shades; an alkaline modifier gives rich browns. The flowers used alone can give rust, orange and yellow shades, especially with an alum mordant. Bell heather (*Erica cinerea*) can also be used in the dye pot. Use 150% dyestuff.

Colours from Calluna vulgaris flowering tops
Left: Br.NM, Gr.NM; Centre from top: AM, NM, NM+A, NM+C, NM+I;
Right: tannin(W), tannin(B)

Centaurea nigra Knapweed

Knapweed

Knapweed is a common perennial wild plant, which also makes an attractive garden plant, especially as it is loved by bees and some butterflies. It flowers for a long period in the summer and into the autumn, particularly if the dead flower heads are removed regularly. These can be dried and used later in the dye pot when the rest of the plant is harvested. Knapweed is mentioned in several dye books as having been used in Scotland as a source of yellow dye. The whole plant top can be used in the dye pot and gives a variety of yellow, tan and green shades. Knapweed gives a bright yellow if used with an alum mordant and a soft mustard yellow colour if used without an alum mordant. An alkaline modifier intensifies the colour, and iron and copper modifiers give pretty moss green shades. Using an alkaline modifier on unmordanted grey fibres dyed in knapweed gives a deep moss green. Use 150% to 200% dyestuff.

Colours from knapweed plant tops and flowers
Left: Br.NM+A, Gr.NM+A;
Centre from top: AM, RL, NM, NM+A, NM+C, NM+I, NM+A+I;
Right: tannin(W), tannin(B), tannin(B)+A

Chamaemelum nobile Chamomile

Chamaemelum nobile

The native British chamomile *Chamaemelum nobile* is the variety of chamomile sold widely for herbal teas. It is an attractive pleasantly scented perennial plant and is sometimes used as lawn chamomile. It contains many of the same dye pigments as dyer's chamomile, *Anthemis tinctoria* (see page 56), although it does not always give the same colours as dyer's chamomile. For my experiments I used only the dried chamomile flower heads but the green leaves can also be added to the dye bath and do not significantly affect the colours achieved. The flowers can give a bright orange/rust colour when used with an alum mordant. If used without an alum mordant, chamomile flowers give shades of tan, which can be enhanced by the use of modifiers. An alkaline modifier gives a pretty green, a copper modifier gives a yellow-green and an iron modifier gives a soft moss green. Use 100% to 150% dyestuff.

Colours from chamomile flowers
Left: Br.NM, Gr.NM; Centre from top: AM, RL, NM, NM+A, NM+C, NM+I;
Right: tannin(W), tannin(B)

65

Cornus sanguinea Common Dogwood

Common dogwood

Cornus sanguinea is a common tree or hedge shrub, which can spread rapidly to form dense groves. The prehistoric archer, known as 'Ötzi the Iceman', discovered in 1991 on the border between Italy and Austria, was carrying arrows made from dogwood.

The leaves and berries of dogwood can be used in the dye pot. When used without an alum mordant, the leaves give shades of tan; an alkaline modifier intensifies the colour, and iron and copper modifiers give soft green shades. A tannin mordant gives deeper colours and an alum mordant produces a yellow-tan. If used on grey wool fibres and if an alkaline and then an iron modifier are applied, dogwood leaves give interesting rich brown-green tones. Dogwood berries should be ripe and black before they are used in the dye pot; they are best used with an alum mordant, when they give yellow shades. Use 150% to 200% dyestuff for both leaves and berries.

Colours from dogwood leaves
Left: Br.NM, Gr.NM; Centre from top: AM, NM, NM+A, NM+C, NM+I, NM+A+I;
Right: tannin(B)

Dahlia spp. Dahlia *

Dahlia flowers

Dahlias are native to Central America and originated in the mountainous areas of Mexico and Columbia. They are the national flower of Mexico. Dahlias are beautiful showy garden plants and can be raised from seed as annuals and used as bedding plants, or grown from tubers for planting in borders. To grow dahlias as annual bedding plants, sow the seeds indoors in individual pots in early spring, several weeks before the last frost, then plant the seedlings out in their flowering positions in late spring, when all danger of frost is over. To grow dahlias from tubers, plant these out four inches deep in their flowering site in mid-spring after the last frosts. Dahlia tubers can often be left in the ground after the plants have flowered and should then shoot again the following year. Otherwise, dig up the tubers in the autumn then spread them out on wire racks to dry before storing them in paper sacks in a cool, dark, dry place. They can then be replanted the next spring when they have started to form shoots. Dahlias will thrive in any well-drained, fertile soil and they need protection from slugs and snails. All the flowers give similar colours in the dye pot, with the exception of the white flowers which do not produce much dye colour. Dahlia leaves can also be used for dyeing and I prefer to keep the flowers and leaves separate, rather than making a dye bath of both together, as they give different colours. Both leaves and flowers can be used fresh or dried for later use and I usually collect the flower heads when I dead-head the plants and dry them ready to use when I have enough for a dye bath. I tend to wait until the plants have finished flowering before I harvest any leaves. Dahlia leaves give various soft shades of green, mustard and tan and dahlia flowers give a range of rust and orange colours. The brightest orange colours are achieved with an alum mordant followed by an alkaline modifier. Without an alum mordant, the colours are less brilliant and more mustard in tone but the use of an alkaline modifier gives a rust colour and iron and copper modifiers give shades of khaki. Rich olive greens can be achieved on grey fibres, especially if an iron modifier is used. Use 200% dyestuff for dahlia leaves and 100% to 150% for dahlia flowers.

The first two photos below show 28 samples from one dye bath of dahlia flowers

From left: AM, Gr.AM, AM+A, Gr.AM+A, AM+C, Gr.AM+C, AM+I, Gr.AM+I

Left: Br.NM, Br.NM+A, Gr.NM, Gr.NM+A; Centre from top: NM, RL, NM+A, RL+A, NM+C, RL+C, NM+I, RL+I; Right: tannin(W), tannin(W)+A, tannin (W)+C, tannin(W)+I, tannin(B), tannin(B)+A, tannin(B)+C, tannin(B)+I

Colours from dahlia leaves
Left: Br.NM, Gr.NM; Centre from top: AM, NM, NM+A, NM+C, NM+I, NM+A+I; Right: tannin(B)

Epilobium spp. Willow Herb

Epilobium hirsutum

Several species of *Epilobium* are common wild plants. They include great willow herb, *Epilobium hirsutum*, small-flowered willow herb, *Epilobium parviflorum*, and rose bay willow herb, *Epilobium angustifolium*, also known as *Chamerion angustifolium* and sometimes called "Fireweed" because it colonises burnt sites. Willow herb does not seem to be a widely used source of dye colour in the UK but its use as a dye plant has been recorded in Norway. The whole plant top can be harvested for the dye pot and should be simmered for about an hour to extract the dye colour. For my tests I used *Epilobium hirsutum*, which gives a pretty green-yellow with an alum mordant. Without an alum mordant the colours are pale unless an alkaline modifier is used. Iron and copper modifiers give soft grey-greens. The colours from willow herb on brown and grey wool are particularly attractive if an alkaline modifier is used after dyeing. Use 150% to 200% dyestuff.

Colours from great willow herb
Left: Br.NM+A, Gr.NM+A; Centre from top: AM, NM, NM+A, NM+C, NM+I, NM+A+I;
Right: tannin(B), tannin(B)+A

69

Equisetum arvense Horsetail

Field horsetail

Horsetail can be described as a "living fossil", as it is the only remaining genus in the entire class of *Equisetopsida* and has survived since the Carboniferous age millions of years ago. It is a perennial non-flowering plant, which reproduces by spores rather than seeds. Horsetail is regarded in some regions as a noxious weed and gardeners particularly dislike it because the rhizomes are extremely difficult to dig out of the ground. It has a long history of medicinal uses, dating back to ancient Greek and Roman medicine. The whole plant top, either fresh or dried, can be used in the dye pot, both with or without an alum mordant. When used with an alum mordant horsetail gives yellows; without an alum mordant the yellows achieved are pale but an alkaline modifier deepens the colour and gives attractive greens if used on brown and grey fibres. Iron and copper modifiers give soft greens. Use 150% to 200% dyestuff.

Colours from horsetail
Left: Br.NM+A, Gr.NM+A; Centre from top: AM, NM, NM+A, NM+C, NM+I;
Right: tannin(B)

Eucalyptus spp. Eucalyptus *

Leaves of Eucalyptus gunnii   *Bark of Eucalyptus gunnii*

There are numerous species of eucalyptus, which are native to Australia but have been introduced worldwide. Eucalyptus trees can grow to huge heights if not regularly pruned but some species can also be grown in large pots and this will restrict their growth. Eucalyptus trees often shed their bark, so you may find fallen bark on the ground beneath the trees. The leaves and the bark of eucalyptus can be used successfully without an alum mordant and give a wide range of shades, from rich browns and reds to yellows and greens, depending on the growing conditions and the individual species used. For my tests I used *Eucalyptus gunnii*, which is the species most commonly grown in Britain. In my experience both the bark and the leaves of this species tend to give colours in the gold, yellow and tan range. However, if the growing conditions are right and the pH of the dye bath is not too alkaline, *Eucalyptus gunnii* leaves can sometimes apparently give orange and red colours.

The method for making a dye bath is the same for both the leaves and the bark, and both are best left to soak overnight before being simmered to make the dye bath. The bark and the leaves can be used together in the dye bath but I prefer to keep them separate. Chop the plant pieces as small as possible and then pour boiling water over them. The soaking water and the dye bath should be slightly acidic and the pH value should be about pH5 or pH6. Add 2 teaspoons of clear vinegar to the soaking water and check the pH before adding more vinegar if necessary. The plant pieces should be left to soak overnight in this slightly acidic water. Then simmer the leaves or bark in this soaking water for 45 minutes to an hour and strain off the dye solution. Add the fibres and heat for 45 minutes but keep the dye bath just below a simmer. Allow the fibres to cool in the dye bath, preferably overnight, then remove them and rinse them. Use 150% to 200% dyestuff for both the bark and the leaves.

Colours from Eucalyptus gunnii leaves
Left: Br.NM, Gr.NM; Centre from top: AM, NM, NM+A, NM+C, NM +I;
Right: tannin(B)

Colours from Eucalyptus gunnii bark
Samples as above for the leaves

Eupatorium cannabinum Hemp Agrimony

Hemp agrimony

Hemp agrimony is a common perennial wild plant which is attractive to butterflies, and the whole plant top can be used in the dye pot. It is also an attractive garden plant but as it spreads rapidly it is perhaps less suitable for small gardens. Harvest the whole plant top as the flowers begin to fade and simmer it for 45 minutes to an hour to extract the dye colour. Strain off the dye solution, add the fibres and simmer them for 45 minutes. Leave the fibres to cool in the dye bath, preferably overnight, then remove them and rinse well. Hemp agrimony gives soft shades of beige if used without an alum mordant and light tan colours with a tannin mordant. Alkaline and copper modifiers give soft greens and an iron modifier gives grey-green. If an alum mordant is used, the colour is brighter and yellower. Use 100% to 150% dyestuff.

Colours from hemp agrimony plant tops
Left: Br.NM, Gr.NM; Centre from top: AM, NM, NM+A, NM+C, NM+I
NM+A+I; Right: tannin (B)

73

Fagus spp. Beech

Beech leaves in spring

Fagus sylvatica is the species of beech considered native to Britain, although there is some recent evidence to suggest it may not have arrived until around 4000 BCE. In the north of England beech is sometimes classified as non-native and removed from "native" woodland. Beech leaves can be used successfully in the dye pot without an alum mordant and give attractive warm shades of tan and brown. They can be used fresh or dried but for my tests I used fresh leaves. To make a dye bath, first pour boiling water over the leaves and leave them to soak overnight. Then simmer them for an hour, strain off the dye solution, add the fibres and simmer for 45 minutes to an hour. A tannin mordant enhances the colours and an alum mordant gives a rust-brown. An alkaline modifier gives a warm rust-brown, a copper modifier gives a softer rust-brown and an iron modifier gives a greenish tone. Use 150% dyestuff.

Colours from beech leaves
Left: Br.NM, Gr.NM; Centre from top: AM, NM, NM+A, NM+C, NM+I;
Right: tannin(W), tannin(B)

Frangula alnus Alder Buckthorn (formerly known as *Rhamnus frangula*)

Alder buckthorn leaves

Alder buckthorn is a perennial small tree or shrub. It prefers wet soils and is one of only two food plants used by the Brimstone butterfly. The leaves, bark and berries of alder buckthorn can be used in the same way as those of buckthorn, *Rhamnus spp.* (see page 111) and give similar colours. Use 150% dyestuff for the leaves and 80% to 100% dyestuff for the bark and the berries.

Colours from alder buckthorn bark
Left: Br.NM, Gr.NM; Centre from top: NM, NM+A, NM+C, NM+I;
Right: tannin(B)

Colours from alder buckthorn leaves
Samples as above plus centre top AM

Fraxinus spp. Ash

Leaves of Fraxinus excelsior

All species of ash can be used for dyeing and tend to produce soft, muted shades. Sadly, in many parts of Europe the European ash, *Fraxinus excelsior*, has recently succumbed to disease and healthy ash trees may be difficult to find. Ash leaves and bark and also the flowers have been reported as being used for dyeing in the past. If used without an alum mordant, the leaves and bark of the ash give pale yellow and beige shades; an alum mordant produces deeper, yellower shades. An alkaline modifier intensifies the colours from the leaves, which give soft green shades with iron and copper modifiers. Ash bark should be soaked for several days before being simmered to extract the dye colour. It gives similar colours to those from the leaves, and browns can be achieved if an iron modifier is used. Ash flowers give soft yellow-green shades with an alum mordant. Use at least 150% dyestuff for all parts of ash.

Colours from ash leaves
Left: Br.NM+A, Gr.NM+A; Centre from top: AM, NM, NM+A, NM+C, NM+I;
Right: tannin(W), tannin(B)

Galium mollugo Hedge Bedstraw

Hedge bedstraw

Before the introduction of dyer's madder, *Rubia tinctorum*, dyers in Britain relied on native sources of red, such as various species of *Galium*. *Galium mollugo* (also known as *Galium album*) is a perennial wild plant and can be grown from seed as described for *Rubia tinctorum* (see page 117). The roots are the parts used for dyeing; they can be used fresh or dried but they should not be harvested until the plants are at least three years old. Wait until the tops have died down then dig deeply to reach the thickest roots. To make a dye bath from hedge bedstraw roots, follow the instructions given for *Galium verum* (page 79) or use the alkaline extraction method (see page 32). Hedge bedstraw roots give shades of coral, orange and rust on alum-mordanted fibres and paler shades if used without an alum mordant. An alkaline modifier intensifies the colours and iron and copper modifiers make the shades browner. Use at least 200% dyestuff.

Colours from Galium mollugo
Left from top: AM, NM, AM+A, NM+A;
Right from left to right: tannin(W), tannin(B), 3 skeins from exhaust dye baths (AM)

77

Galium odoratum Sweet Woodruff

Sweet woodruff

Galium odoratum is a perennial wild plant with fragrant white flowers in late spring. It makes an attractive garden plant, which spreads rapidly and seems happy in both sun and shade, although it prefers partial shade. Plants can often be purchased from suppliers of native wild plants and woodruff can also be grown from seed as described for *Rubia tinctorum* (see page 117). The roots are the parts used for dyeing; they should not be harvested until the plants are at least three years old and they can be used fresh, or dried and stored for use later. Wait until the tops have died down then dig deeply to make sure you harvest the thickest roots. Wash them well and then process and use the roots as described on page 79 for *Galium verum*. They give shades very similar to those from *Galium mollugo*, but less bright, and react in a similar way to the modifiers. The colour from sweet woodruff roots can also be extracted and applied using the alkaline extraction method (see page 32). Use at least 200% dyestuff.

Colours from Galium odoratum
Left from top: AM, NM, AM+A, NM+A; Right: tannin(W), tannin(B)

Galium verum Lady's Bedstraw

Lady's bedstraw

Lady's bedstraw is a perennial wild plant with small yellow flowers and it was the main source of red dye in Scotland where it grows widely, especially in sandy coastal soils. It can be grown from seed as described for *Rubia tinctorum* (see page 117). The roots are the parts used for dyeing and they should not be harvested until the plants are at least three years old. To make a dye bath, wash the roots then pour boiling water over them and leave them to soak overnight. Then simmer them for about an hour and strain off the liquid. Add the fibres and heat to just below simmering point. Hold at this temperature for at least an hour then turn off the heat. Leave the fibres to soak in the dye bath overnight then remove them and rinse. Lady's bedstraw roots give shades of coral, orange and rust. The colour can also be extracted and applied using the alkaline extraction method (see page 32). Use at least 200% dyestuff.

Colours from lady's bedstraw
Left: Br.NM, Gr.NM; Centre from top: AM, NM, NM+A, NM+C, NM+I;
Right: tannin (W), tannin(B)

Genista tinctoria Dyer's Broom

Dyer's broom before flowering   *Dyer's broom in flower*

Dyer's broom is a perennial shrub which produces spikes of small, vivid yellow flowers at the tips of its branches from early summer. It has a long history as a dye plant and has been in use since the Iron Age, if not even longer. *Genista tinctoria* contains many of the same dye pigments as dyer's weld (*Reseda luteola*) and is one of the fastest yellow dyes. Excavations at the Viking age site in York in northern England produced plant remains containing dyer's broom, indicating that it was used in the Anglo-Scandinavian era in the ninth to eleventh centuries. Dyer's broom was used widely in the north west of England and, when overdyed with woad, it was used to make the colour known as 'Kendal Green'. It was also the *"planta genista"* worn as an emblem by the Plantagenet kings of England; the name of this dynasty dates from the fifteenth century and comes from the nickname *"Plantegenest"* given in the twelfth century to its founder, Geoffrey of Anjou.

Dyer's broom plants can frequently be purchased from nurseries or garden centres but it is not difficult to grow your own. Soak the seeds overnight in warm water, then sow them in individual pots either in the autumn and leave them outside over the winter, or outdoors in mid-spring. Plant them out in late spring in their flowering positions when they are several inches tall and look strong and healthy. Although they may only grow slowly in the first year, they should flower in the second season and will continue to flourish for many years. Dyer's broom likes full sun and ordinary, light, well-drained soil. Most succeed well in poor soil and hot dry sites. The shoots can be harvested for the dye pot at any time during the growing season. Cutting the plants back will encourage new growth and make them bushier. I usually cut off all the first crop of flowering stems as the little flowers begin to fade and then harvest another batch later in the year when I prune the bushes. The leaves, stems and flowers can be mixed together in the dye pot and can be used fresh or dried. With an alum mordant, dyer's broom gives clear bright yellows and paler yellows without an alum mordant. However, if unmordanted fibres are dyed in dyer's broom and then an alkaline modifier is applied, the yellows achieved can be almost as bright as those from an alum mordant. A copper modifier gives a soft lime green and an iron modifier gives a moss green. Dyer's broom also gives attractive shades of mossy green on grey and brown wool, especially with an alkaline modifier. Tannin mordants can give a range of tan and mustard colours, which become rich grey-greens if copper or iron modifiers are used. The colour from dyer's broom can also be extracted and applied using the alkaline extraction method (see page 32). Use 150% dyestuff.

Colours from fresh dyer's broom
Left: Br.NM+A, Br.NM+A+I, Gr.NM+A, Gr.NM+A+I;
Centre from top: AM, CL, RL, NM, NM+A, NM+A+C, NM+I;
Right: tannin(W), tannin(W)+A, tannin(B), tannin(B)+A, tannin(B)+C, tannin (B)+I

Colours from dried dyer's broom
From top: AM+A, AM, AM+I, AM+C

81

Hedera helix Ivy

Ivy leaves and berries

Ivy is a common hardy, evergreen climber or creeper and the leaves and berries can both be used in the dye pot, either together or separately. Leaves can be gathered throughout the year and the berries are best harvested when they are black. Both leaves and berries will give stronger colours if the plant materials are left in the pot during dyeing but tie them into a net bag or they may be difficult to remove from the fibres afterwards. Chop the leaves and mash the berries up in hot water and then simmer them for about an hour until they are soft. Add the materials to be dyed and simmer until a good depth of colour is reached. An alum mordant gives yellows; without an alum mordant both the leaves and the berries give pale tans, which become deeper with an alkaline modifier. Use 200% dyestuff for both leaves and berries.

Colours from ivy leaves and berries mixed
Left: Br.NM, Gr.NM; Centre from top: AM, NM, NM+A, NM+C, NM+I;
Right: tannin(W), tannin(B)

Humulus lupulus Common Hop

Golden hop leaves

Hops

The hop plant is a vigorous perennial climber, which makes an attractive garden plant, especially in its golden-leaved form. It is also frequently found in the wild. Hops, also called seed cones or strobiles, are the female flowers, which are an important ingredient in beer and are also used in herbal medicine. Both yellow and hazel-coloured dyes were reportedly made from hops in the eighteenth century. The whole plant top, with or without flowers, can be used in the dye pot and gives attractive colours without an alum mordant, especially if modifiers are applied. If hop flowers are used fresh, rather than dried, and if they are boiled long enough to extract the colour, a brownish red can often be obtained from them on wool with or without an alum mordant. For my experiments I used dried hops. Use 150% to 200% dyestuff.

Colours from dried hops
Left: Br.NM+A, Gr.NM+A; Centre from top: AM, NM, NM+A,
NM+C, NM+I; Right: tannin(W)

Hypericum spp. St. John's Wort

Hypericum perforatum

Hypericum "Hidcote"

Perforate St. John's Wort (*Hypericum perforatum*) is a native wild plant that makes an attractive perennial garden plant and is easy to grow from seed. Sow the seeds indoors in early spring or outdoors in late spring and plant the seedlings out as soon as they are well grown. Perforate St. John's Wort likes full sun but will tolerate partial shade and will thrive in most average garden soils. It is trouble-free, tough and long-lived. It can be propagated by lifting and dividing established plants in spring, although it spreads of its own accord anyway and self-seeds readily. If the whole plant tops are used in the dye pot, they give a pretty yellow-green colour with an alum mordant and tan shades if used without an alum mordant. The modifiers enhance the colours; an alkaline modifier gives a pink tone, and copper and iron modifiers give shades of brown. The flower heads of Perforate St. John's Wort, if used alone in the dye pot and in the correct sequence, produce a series of four different shades on wool fibres. First, simmer the flower heads until the dye liquid is deep red and strain off the liquid. Add an alum-mordanted skein to the dye bath and simmer for about 20 minutes until the skein becomes green. Remove it and add an unmordanted wool skein to the same dye bath. Simmer for an hour until this skein becomes reddish-maroon. Remove the second skein and add an alum-mordanted or unmordanted skein. Leave this skein to soak overnight to absorb the remaining green and red dye and become a browner colour. Remove this skein and heat the dye bath, then add an alum-mordanted skein. Simmer until this skein becomes yellow or gold. Use 150% to 200% dyestuff for both methods.

The species of *Hypericum* more commonly grown as garden plants (for example *Hypericum "Hidcote"* shown above) can also be used in the dye pot. For my tests, I used the pruned tops from *Hypericum "Hidcote"* shrubs but without the flower heads. Use 150% to 200% dyestuff.

Colours from Hypericum perforatum
Left: Br.NM, Gr.NM; Centre from top: AM, NM, NM+A, NM+C,
NM+I; Right: tannin(W), tannin(B)

Colours from Hypericum "Hidcote" tops without flowers
Left: Br.NM+A, Gr.NM+A; Centre from top: NM+A (silk), AM, NM, NM+C, NM+I;
Right: tannin(W)+A, tannin(B)+A

Isatis tinctoria Woad *

Woad in flower

Woad is native to Central and Southern Europe and parts of Asia and was probably introduced into Britain when farming developed in the Neolithic period. Before the introduction of indigo (*Indigofera spp.*) from the East in the sixteenth century, woad was the source of blue dye in Europe. It was one of the earliest dyes used and it seems to be the dye most frequently found on early European textile fragments, including some from the Iron Age. However, it is likely that woad was in use in Europe from an even earlier date.

The distinction often made between indigo and woad can be misleading, as woad is one of many indigo-bearing plants, all of which contain the same indigo blue dye pigments. In some of the recipes below, the term woad-indigo is used to indicate woad and other indigo-bearing plants. However, the blue colouring matter is present in woad leaves in much lower concentrations, so *Indigofera spp.* eventually superseded woad. Indigo-bearing plants occur in many parts of the world and most of the indigo powder available commercially comes from species of *Indigofera*. Indigo from woad (*Isatis tinctoria*) can now also be obtained in powder form and is used in the same way as other indigo powders.

The sources of indigo blue most usually grown by dyers are woad (*Isatis tinctoria*) and Japanese Indigo (*Persicaria tinctoria* formerly called *Polygonum tinctorium*). The fresh leaves of both these plants are used in very similar ways to make an indigo vat and both can also be used to give a paler and sometimes less stable blue in a more direct method using only vinegar. No mordant is required for blues from indigo-bearing plants.

Woad belongs to the cabbage or *Brassicaceae* family and is extremely easy to grow. It is a biennial plant which forms leaves in its first year and then flowers and goes to seed the next. The first year's leaves contain the greatest quantity of blue dye pigment and they are best used fresh, as drying them destroys much of the blue dye potential. I have very occasionally managed to get blues from dried leaves but much depends on the time of year that the leaves are harvested for drying, as well as the dyeing method used, and success is rare.

First year leaves

Second year leaves

Woad seeds should be sown outdoors in rows, either in early spring or in early autumn. Sowing seeds at both times will give you usable leaves from late summer through to mid-autumn. Woad has a long tap root and if seedlings are transplanted great care must be taken not to damage the root. The plants should be about 30cm (12in) apart. In its second year of growth woad sends up a tall flowering stem which produces masses of small, vivid yellow flowers. They then develop green, dangling seed pods, which become purple-black as they mature. Second year woad plants are decorative and can be quite spectacular. However, unless you want to use the seeds for dyeing, it is advisable to cut down most of the stems once the plants have flowered and just save one or two stalks for the seeds. Otherwise you may have woad plants growing everywhere the next year.

The leaves should be harvested in their first year of growth, ideally from late summer to mid-autumn. If you harvest them too early, they will not have developed enough blue pigment and leaves gathered too late in the year may have lost some of their blue dye potential. However, I have managed to obtain blues from woad leaves harvested throughout the year, even sometimes in the depths of winter, so it is always worth experimenting at different times of the year, although success cannot be guaranteed. If blues should occasionally prove elusive, leaves gathered at any time of the year will produce shades of pinkish tan, whether they are fresh or dried.

No mordant is required for blues from woad-indigo. The recipes given below should dye up to 500g (1lb) of fibres a medium blue.

IMPORTANT: Read the safety notes on page 153 carefully before embarking on dyeing with woad or other indigo-bearing plants. Take particular care with sodium hydrosulphite and other reducing agents; do not pour water on to them but add them slowly to water. Always wear rubber gloves when dyeing with woad or other indigo-bearing plants.

Dyeing with woad/indigo in powder form

METHOD 1 The Hydrosulphite Vat

1 Dissolve 4 teaspoons of washing soda or soda ash in 4 to 6 tablespoons of boiling water and cool slightly. Then add 3–4 teaspoons of woad/indigo powder to this solution and mix it very well to a smooth paste, adding more water if necessary. Make sure no gritty particles remain unmixed. Leave it to stand for 15 minutes.

2 Put enough water to make the vat into a stainless steel dye pot and heat to 50 C/120 F. This is as about as hot as your hand will tolerate. Make sure the temperature does not exceed 60 C/140 F.

3 Add approximately 20–25g (1oz) of reducing agent (sodium hydrosulphite [Hydros], Spectralite or Thiox) and stir very gently. Leave for 1–2 minutes then very gently stir in the woad/indigo paste solution, making sure not to create any air bubbles as you do so.

4 Put a lid on the pot and, keeping the temperature constant, leave the vat to stand for 30–45 minutes or until the liquid below the surface has changed from blue to greenish yellow in colour. (The surface may still appear blue because it is in contact with oxygen in the air.) If after 45 minutes the liquid still appears blue, add a little more reducing agent and leave it for a further 5–10 minutes. The pH value should be 9 or 10, so add a little more soda ash if the pH value is below 9.

5 Gently enter the wetted yarn or fabric, remembering to squeeze out any excess water first. Do not put more materials in the vat than will lie easily below the surface, as any sections above the surface may become blotchy. Leave the materials in the vat for 5–20 minutes, depending on the depth of colour you want.

6 Remove the materials very gently, making sure they do not drip into the vat. Then immerse them in a bowl or bucket of clear water and move them around to remove any spots of undissolved indigo, which may cause blotches.

7 Expose the materials to the air for 20 minutes or so to allow the blue colour to develop fully.

8 You can build up the depth of colour by re-dipping the materials in the vat and airing them until you achieve the desired shade.

9 If the vat begins to turn blue, add a little more reducing agent but only enough to turn it greenish yellow again.

10 When you have the desired depth of colour, rinse the materials thoroughly several times, then wash them well and rinse again.

This vat can often be kept going for several days, if you put clingfilm or plastic wrap over the surface to keep out oxygen from the air. If it cools down overnight, just heat it gently in the morning and add a little more reducing agent if the liquid below the surface appears blue.

When the materials no longer take up any more colour, the vat is exhausted and you will need to make a fresh one for further batches. I usually put a final skein in the vat and leave it overnight to soak up any remaining colour. Before disposal, exhaust any remaining reducing agent by whisking or agitating the vat to incorporate oxygen from the air. It can then be poured away down the drain or on the ground.

Colour Run Remover in powder form contains sodium hydrosulphite and can be used instead of reducing agent in step 3. It also contains washing soda, so use only 2 teaspoons of washing soda/soda ash in step 1. Do not use Colour Run Remover in liquid form, as it is not effective in woad/indigo vats.

Results from a woad/indigo powder hydrosulphite vat

METHOD 2 The 1-2-3 Lime/Fructose Vat

This vat was developed by Michel Garcia, a bio-chemist and expert dyer who has been researching indigo dyeing for many years and who has developed indigo vats that are simple to make and ready to use in a short space of time. It gives medium blues.

Slaked lime (calcium hydroxide) is also known as builders' lime and can usually be purchased from builders' merchants; it can also be found for sale on the internet. It should be handled with care, as it is an irritant and can cause injury if it comes into contact with the eyes. Do not pour water on to it but add it slowly to water. (The main active component of garden or agricultural lime is usually calcium carbonate (chalk), which is not effective in 1-2-3 vats.)

Fructose can usually be purchased from health food shops and may also be available in some supermarkets.

The 1-2-3 vat is so called because of the proportions of the ingredients used: one part woad/indigo powder, two parts slaked lime (calcium hydroxide) and three parts fructose. This means that for 10g woad/indigo powder you would need 20g calcium hydroxide and 30g fructose; for 20g indigo powder you would need 40g calcium hydroxide and 60g fructose and so on.

To make the vat, start by putting hot water (about 50 C/120 F and no hotter than 60 C/140 F) into a dye pot or heatproof strong glass jar. Mix the woad/indigo powder with hot water to make a smooth paste, making sure no gritty particles remain unmixed. Add this woad/indigo solution to the hot water in the pot or jar then carefully stir in the calcium hydroxide. Finally add the fructose and stir well. The vat may take up to 45 minutes to be ready to use but can sometimes be ready in as little as 5 minutes. It can then be used in the same way as other indigo vats. Proceed as for Method 1 from step 5 (see page 89).

1. The 1-2-3 vat plus ingredients

2. The 1-2-3 vat ready to use

3. The fibres in the 1-2-3 vat

4. Fibres dyed in a 1-2-3 vat

METHOD 3 The Urine Vat

This is an ancient way of using woad/indigo powder and when it is successful it can be very satisfying because it makes use of a readily available natural product. It requires constant heat over a longish period and produces a strong odour.

Stale urine contains both ammonia (an alkali) and also the bacteria necessary for removing oxygen from the vat. You will need to collect enough urine to make the vat and it should be 2 to 3 weeks old before you use it. If possible, leave it open to the air during storage, as bacteria from the air will assist in reducing the indigo. Make sure you store it in a clearly labelled container. When the urine is ready, put it in a stainless steel or heatproof glass pot with a well-fitting lid and heat to 50 C/120 F.

Dissolve 1 teaspoon of washing soda or soda ash in hot water, then stir in 3–4 teaspoons of woad/indigo powder as described for Method 1. Stir this indigo paste into the stale urine, leave it for a few minutes then check the pH value of the solution. If necessary, add washing soda, soda ash or wood ash water to bring it to pH9. Then put the lid on firmly and leave it in a warm place for one to two days. To maintain a constant temperature, the pot can be left on the type of electric heater used for keeping food warm or placed in a warm sunny spot, padded round with sawdust or polystyrene granules to maintain the heat, especially if the surrounding temperature drops at night. The pot can also be placed inside a larger container filled with hot water which will need to be replaced regularly to keep the pot warm.

After 24–36 hours the solution should be greenish yellow. To test it, add a small sample of wool, leave it in the vat for 5–10 minutes then remove it. If the wool doesn't turn blue on exposure to the air, leave the vat for a little longer and then test again. It may take up to 3–4 days for the vat to be ready for use. When the vat is ready, add the materials to be dyed and proceed as described for Method 1, from step 5 onwards (page 89).

METHOD 4 The Fermentation Vat

If carefully monitored, this vat can be very successful and its odour is less unpleasant than that of the urine and yeast vats (see page 98 for details of the yeast vat). To make a fermentation vat you will need:
Woad/indigo powder
Washing soda, soda ash or wood ash water as the source of alkali
10 to 15g (approximately ½oz) bran
10 to 15g (approximately ½oz) madder root
3 or 4 chopped dates to "feed" the vat
pH papers to check the alkalinity.

Make a woad/indigo paste solution with washing soda as described in Method 1, step 1. Fill a stainless steel pot with water then heat it to 50 C/120 F (as hot as your hand will tolerate) and stir in the indigo paste. Check the pH which should be pH9. If necessary add more washing soda, soda ash or wood ash water until pH9 is reached. Add 10g each of bran and madder, stir well and put a lid on the pot. Then put it on a hot-plate, such as those used for keeping food warm, to maintain a constant temperature. Don't let the temperature exceed 60 C/140 F. Stir the vat every 2 hours or so. If the fermentation is slow (i.e. if nothing much seems to be happening after 12–18 hours), add 2 chopped dates and a little more bran and madder. Check the alkalinity with pH papers from time to time and if necessary add more washing soda, soda ash or wood ash water to maintain pH9. Add another chopped date to maintain fermentation, especially overnight or if the vat starts to turn blue. If the correct temperature and a level of pH9 are maintained, the liquid in the vat should eventually become greenish-yellow in colour but this may take up to 3 or 4 days. The vat is then ready to use. Add the fibres and proceed as described for Method 1, from step 5 onwards (see page 89).

Samples from a fermentation vat

Dyeing with woad balls

Woad balls

In the past, woad was usually traded in the form of woad balls or couched woad. Woad balls were made by crushing the woad leaves to a pulp between rollers, draining off any excess liquid, then rolling the pulp into balls, which were laid on racks to be dried. If woad was traded as balls, they then had to be processed further into couched woad before they were ready for dyeing. To make couched woad, the balls were pulverised, sprinkled with water and left to ferment. During this period, the mass was turned frequently and large lumps were broken up. Finally, this crumbly substance, known as couched woad, was dried and packed into barrels, ready to be sent off for sale. Although woad powder has largely replaced woad balls or couched woad, it is occasionally possible to purchase woad balls, which can be used to make a fermentation vat as described above or used as described below.

Use at least two woad balls and remember that they must remain in the vat throughout except during the initial whisking process. The woad balls must first be crushed or broken into very small pieces and you may need to use a hammer or a mallet as they can be very hard. Then pour a little cold water over them (just enough to cover them) before adding enough boiling water to make the vat. Leave the crushed woad balls to soak for about an hour then strain off the liquid. Add enough washing soda, soda ash or wood ash water to turn the liquid from brown to green and whisk vigorously or pour the liquid from one container to another for about 15 minutes to introduce oxygen. The liquid may not produce blue froth but this is normal when using woad balls. After whisking for about 15 minutes, return the pieces of woad ball to the liquid, stir well and then pour the liquid, plus woad ball pieces, into a stainless steel pot. Heat gently to about 50 C/120 F and then add 2–3 teaspoons of sodium hydrosulphite (or alternative reducing agent) to remove the oxygen. After about 10–15 minutes the vat should be ready to use. Use the vat as described above for woad/indigo in powder form Method 1, from step 5 onwards (see page 89).

This vat can usually be kept working for several days and the colours on the second and third days are often just as strong as those on the first day, probably because leaving the woad ball pieces in the vat allows the blue to continue to develop as time progresses. This vat does not look like the usual woad or indigo vats; the colour of the liquid is a murky brown/yellow. After a while a blue metallic sheen may appear on the surface, only to disappear again later.

Wool in the woad ball vat

Wool emerging from the vat

Dyeing with fresh woad leaves

METHOD 1 The Hydrosulphite Vat

Use 200% to 300% fresh woad leaves for deep blues initially. Paler blues will be achieved as the vat becomes gradually weaker.

Tear or cut the leaves into small pieces and put them into a pot or a heatproof plastic bucket. Pour at least enough boiling water over them to make the vat and make sure all the leaves are well covered. Then leave them to steep for about an hour or so. Then strain off the sherry-coloured liquid, squeezing the leaves well to extract all the dye potential. Don't throw the leaves away immediately, because they can be used later on for a further dye bath to achieve a pinkish-tan colour, if desired.

Make sure the liquid has cooled to 50 C/120 F, which is about as hot as a hand can tolerate, then add just enough alkali, in the form of wood ash water or washing soda/soda ash, to the strained-off liquid to turn it from brown to green. Now you must introduce oxygen to convert this solution into indigo blue. Do this either by whisking the liquid vigorously or by pouring it from one container to another. The froth that forms should start to turn blue after a few minutes. If this doesn't happen, add a little more alkali and keep on whisking or pouring until the froth has turned blue and is beginning to turn green or yellow again. Let the froth subside a little, then put the liquid into a dye pot and heat it to 50 C/120 F. Don't let it get any hotter but keep the temperature constant if you can. Sprinkle 2–3 teaspoons of reducing agent (sodium hydrosulphite [Hydros], Spectralite, Thiox or powdered Colour Run Remover) over the surface to remove the oxygen and leave the vat to stand for about 30 minutes. After this time the liquid in the vat should have become greenish yellow in colour; if the liquid still appears blue, add a little more reducing agent and leave the vat for a further 10–15 minutes. When the liquid in the vat looks greenish yellow, it is ready to use.

Add the wetted fibres gently, without splashes or bubbles, and follow the instructions given above for woad/indigo powder Method 1, from step 5 onwards (see page 89).

Keep on using the vat for successive batches of fibre but don't add too much for later batches, as you will sometimes find that pretty soft pink, lavender and turquoise shades can result as the vat becomes exhausted.

This method can also be used with the fresh leaves of Japanese Indigo (*Persicaria tinctoria/Polygonum tinctorium*) but, instead of pouring boiling water over the leaves, add cold water and heat gradually to simmering point. Then remove the pot from the heat and allow the leaves to steep in the liquid for about an hour. Strain off the liquid, squeezing the leaves well to extract all the dye potential, and continue as for woad leaves above.

Woad leaves soaking in hot water

The blue froth formed by whisking

The skein in the vat after the reducing agent has been added

The skein coming out of the vat and changing colour on exposure to the air

The dyed skein drying

METHOD 2   The Yeast Vat

Use 200% to 300% fresh woad leaves. Tear up the leaves and pour
enough boiling water over them for the vat and to cover them, then leave
them to steep for an hour or so. Meanwhile put some hand-hot water
into a jug, stir in 3 teaspoons of sugar and 4 teaspoons of dried yeast
and leave it until the yeast begins to froth. When the leaves have finished
steeping, make sure the liquid has cooled to 50 C/120 F and gradually

add washing soda or soda ash to bring the solution to pH9 or 10. Don't remove the leaves, which must remain in the vat for this method. Then stir in the yeast solution. The vat must now be kept warm for as long as it takes to turn it greenish-yellow. This vat is usually ready to use after about 36 hours and can be kept going for several days but check the pH regularly and add more soda if necessary to maintain pH9 or 10. Use the vat as described for woad/indigo powder Method 1, from step 5 onwards (see page 89), leaving the fibres in the vat for about 45 minutes to start with. When you remove the materials, immerse them in clear water and move them around to shake out any leaves clinging to the fibres and then air them as usual. This type of vat often produces a variety of shades, ranging from pinks, lavenders, greys and soft greens to blues.

Samples from a yeast vat   *Skein dyed in a urine vat*

METHOD 3 The Urine Vat

Woad leaves can also be used to make a urine vat. Use 200% to 300% fresh leaves.

First collect enough urine to make up half the liquid required for your vat and leave it for 2 to 3 weeks as described on page 92 for the urine vat made from woad/indigo powder. Keep the urine container open to the air if possible, as bacteria from the air will assist in reducing the indigo. When the urine is ready, harvest the woad leaves and follow the instructions given for preparing fresh leaves in Method 1 above, up to and including the whisking or pouring process to convert the liquid to indigo blue. Use only half the quantity of water necessary for your vat, because the other half will be the stale urine. Add the woad solution to the stale urine and heat the mixture to 50 C/120 F. Put it into a container with a well-fitting lid and keep it warm for a week or so, using one of the methods suggested for the woad/indigo powder urine vat. When the liquid has become greenish yellow in colour, the vat is ready to use. To use this vat, follow the instructions given above for woad/indigo powder Method 1, from step 5 onwards (see page 89).

METHOD 4 The Vinegar Method

Use 200% to 300% fresh leaves. This method works particularly well with the leaves of Japanese Indigo (*Persicaria tinctoria/Polygonum tinctorium*) but it can also be used with woad leaves. It gives medium blues which may be less stable than the blues from the more traditional methods of dyeing with woad/indigo. However, this method requires only water and clear 5% vinegar. The vinegar should be added at the rate of about 15ml (approximately 3 teaspoons) clear vinegar per litre of water. Harvest the leaves and process them immediately and as speedily as possible. Chop up the leaves very finely, preferably not using a wooden chopping board, as this may absorb too much of the precious dye solution, or process them in batches with a little water in a liquidiser. Put the chopped leaves into a container and add cool water to which the vinegar has been added. Then knead the leaves very thoroughly for at least 5 minutes, until the liquid is bright green. Strain off the liquid and set it aside. Knead the leaves again in water and vinegar as before, strain off this liquid and add it to the liquid reserved from the first kneading process. Immerse the wetted fibres immediately in the liquid and leave them to soak for about an hour. Then remove them, rinse them in clear water and air them. Leave a small amount of fibres in the liquid overnight to exhaust any remaining dye potential.

Blues from the vinegar vat on wool and silk

Other colours from woad leaves
To obtain tan colours from woad leaves from which the blue dye has been extracted or from leaves that have not first been used for blues, simmer them for about 45 minutes to make the dye bath. Then strain off the liquid, add the fibres, which do not need to be mordanted, and simmer them gently for 30 minutes to an hour. Leave the fibres to cool in the dye bath then remove them and rinse them. This recipe can also be used with the leaves of Japanese Indigo (*Persicaria tinctoria/Polygonum tinctorium*).

Tan colours from woad leaves (NM)

Dyeing with woad seeds

Woad seeds can also be used for dyeing so, if you have a bumper crop, save some seeds to sow for next year's plants and use the rest in the dye pot. Simmer the seeds gently for an hour or so, then strain off the liquid and simmer the materials in it for 30 minutes to an hour. Woad seeds usually produce soft pink and beige colours on unmordanted wool fibres and soft greens on wool fibres mordanted with alum. Use 50% to 100% seeds.

Mature woad seeds

Colours from woad seeds
From top: AM, AM (exhaust), NM

Making woad solution for storage

Although woad leaves are best used fresh for blues, woad liquid once processed can be stored for a year or so for use later. I have successfully stored woad solutions for several years and it is a useful way of using up leaves if you have a bumper crop.

To make the solution follow the instructions given in Method 1 for fresh leaves (page 95) up to and including whisking or pouring to incorporate oxygen. Leave the liquid for a while to allow the froth to settle, then carefully pour it into an airtight container with a well-fitting lid. Fill it up so the liquid overflows slightly, then screw the lid on tightly. The stored woad solution can be used to make a vat by heating it to 50 C/120 F and then adding a reducing agent, as described in Method 1 for fresh woad leaves (page 95). It can also be used to make a urine vat as described on page 99.

Juglans spp. Walnut *

Walnut leaves

Walnuts in their green outer hulls

The Persian or English walnut (*Juglans regia*) is a native of Central Asia and may have been introduced into Britain by the Romans. Other species of walnut are found in various parts of the world and all can be used for dyeing. Walnut dye was used by the Romans, and the Vikings used a solution made from walnut hulls both as a dye and also as an anti-bacterial treatment for clothing. Once the walnut tree had been introduced into Britain, it became a traditional source of dye here from the later Anglo-Saxon period onwards. The leaves and the green outer hulls of the walnut fruits make excellent dyes and can be used successfully without a mordant. (Research carried out by Gill Dalby and presented in her book *Natural Dyes: Fast or Fugitive* indicates that using an alum mordant actually reduces the fastness of colours from walnut leaves.) The leaves give shades ranging from yellows to browns, depending on the time of year they are harvested and whether they are used fresh or dried. Fresh leaves harvested in the summer can give excellent browns, while dried leaves tend to give tan to yellowish shades. An alkaline modifier used with walnut leaves gives a rich brown, while iron and copper modifiers produce soft greens. The outer green hulls or nut casings of the walnut give various depths of brown but the deepest browns come from the fresh green nut cases; once these have been dried they tend to give paler shades. It doesn't matter if the nuts are still in their outer hulls when the dye bath is made but, as they don't add to the dye content, my inclination would be to remove the nuts and reserve them for eating. Simmer the walnut hulls for about an hour to extract the colour and then leave the hulls to soak in the dye liquid for a few days before straining off the dye liquid to make the dye bath. The dye solution, preferably together with the hulls, can be stored for months or even years and storage will increase the strength of the dye. If mould develops, just remove it before straining off and using the dye solution. Use 100% to 150% dyestuff for the leaves and 50% to 100% for the hulls.

Colours from dried walnut hulls
Right: Br.NM, Gr.NM;
Centre from top: AM, NM, NM+A, NM+C, NM+I;
Left: tannin(B)

Colours from dried walnut leaves
Right: Br.NM, Gr.NM; Centre from top: AM, NM, NM+A, NM+C, NM+I;
Right: tannin(W), tannin(B)

Juniperus communis Juniper

Leafy shoots of juniper

Juniper berries

Juniper is a hardy evergreen shrub and is probably best known for its berries, which are used in cooking. Both the berries and the leafy shoots can be used in the dye pot. The berries can be harvested when they are still green or when they have become black and the leafy shoots can be harvested at any time. Both leafy shoots and berries can be used fresh or dried and can be used without an alum mordant. To make a dye bath from the leafy shoots, don't separate the leaves from the twigs, but chop up the whole shoots and simmer them for about an hour or so. Strain off the dye liquid and use it in the usual way. The berries should be well crushed and then boiled fairly vigorously until the liquid is strongly coloured, but keep an eye on the pot and ensure it doesn't boil dry. Then strain off the liquid, add the materials and simmer them for between 30 minutes and an hour. Watch the colour as it develops on the fibres, as simmering for too long can make the shade duller. Both leafy shoots and berries give shades of yellow and khaki and can be mixed together in the dye bath. Use 150% dyestuff for leaves and berries.

Colours from juniper shoots and berries used together
Left: Br.NM+A, Gr.NM+A; Centre from top: AM, NM, NM+A, NM+C, NM+I;
Right: tannin(W), tannin(B)

Malus spp. Apple

Apple leaves and blossom in spring

The leaves and bark of all types of apple trees, including crab apple, can be used in the dye pot. One or two chopped crab apples can also be added to madder dye baths to brighten the colour (see page 123). If harvested in the summer, the leaves of apple trees give rich yellows with an alum mordant. Autumn leaves give browner shades. Pour boiling water over the leaves and leave them to soak overnight before making the dye bath. If used without an alum mordant, the leaves give a very pale yellow, which becomes a soft mustard shade if an alkaline modifier is used. Copper and iron modifiers give delicate greens. The bark of the apple tree can also be used in the dye pot and produces yellow and brown colours. Brighter colours are often achieved if the outer bark is first removed and only the inner bark is used to make the dye bath. Use 150% dyestuff for both leaves and bark.

Colours from apple leaves
Left: Gr.NM; Centre from top: AM, NM, NM+A, NM+C, NM+I;
Right: tannin(B)

Prunus spp. Cherry, Plum, Peach

Wild cherry leaves

Wild cherry bark (Prunus avium)

There are over 400 species of *Prunus* and the leaves and bark of all species can be used for dyeing. With an alum mordant the leaves give yellows; without an alum mordant the leaves give shades of soft tan; an alkaline modifier gives brown tones, and iron and copper modifiers give soft greens. The bark gives mustard yellow with an alum mordant; without an alum mordant the bark gives a range of warm tan and rust-brown shades; an alkaline modifier deepens the colours and an iron modifier gives a soft grey-green. Use 150% to 200% dyestuff for both the leaves and the bark.

Colours from wild cherry leaves (above) and wild cherry bark (below)
Left: Br.NM+A, Gr.NM+A; Centre from top: AM, NM, NM+A, NM+C, NM+I;
Right: tannin(B), tannin(B)+A

Quercus spp. Oak

Quercus robur leaves & acorns

Oak galls

The native British species of oak are *Quercus robur*, the pedunculate or common oak, and *Quercus petraea*, the sessile oak. Other species of oak occur elsewhere and all can be used for dyeing. All parts of the oak are rich in tannin and can be used without an alum mordant. Oak leaves give shades of tan and brown, which become brighter with an alkaline modifier; iron and copper modifiers give soft greens. Oak bark and acorns give dull gold and tan shades, which can be brightened with an alkaline modifier. Oak galls (also called gall nuts or oak apples) are small brown swellings which occur when the gall wasp inserts her eggs into an oak shoot. This stimulates the tree to grow plant tissue around the developing larvae and this becomes the little nut-like gall. Oak galls are rich in tannin and like oak bark they can be used as a tannin mordant (see page 29). A solution made from oak galls and iron sulphate produces a black dye which was used in the past as writing ink. Use 150% dyestuff for oak leaves and acorns, 50% for oak galls and 100% for oak bark.

Colours from acorns
Left: Br.NM, Gr.NM; Centre from top: AM, NM, NM+A, NM+C, NM+I;
Right: tannin(B), tannin(B)+I

Colours from dried oak leaves
Left: Br.NM, Gr.NM; Centre from top: AM, NM, NM+A, NM+C, NM+I;
Right: tannin(W), tannin(B)

Colours from oak bark
Left: Br.NM, Gr.NM; Centre from top: AM, NM, NM+A, NM+C, NM+I;
Right: tannin(B)

Reseda luteola Weld

Weld seedling

Weld in flower

Weld is one of the most ancient of dyes. It has been identified on textile fragments from the Iron Age and there are indications that it may have been in use in the Neolithic period. It gives some of the most light-fast and wash-fast yellow shades, especially when used with a copper modifier. Weld over-dyed with blue from woad produced the colour known as 'Lincoln Green'.

Weld likes an open site and it can often be found on recently turned open ground. If you harvest weld from the wild, cut off the stems just above the lowest two or three side shoots. These will then develop and grow a flowering stalk, producing seeds for the next crop.

Weld is a biennial plant and is easy to grow from seed; if started early enough it will sometimes send up flowering stalks in its first year. It has a long taproot and doesn't always react well to being transplanted, so it may be better to sow seeds outdoors in spring in their growing positions and then thin them out to 20cm (8in) apart when they are large enough to handle. Weld usually forms a flat rosette of leaves in its first year and produces the flowering stalk in the second year. These first year leaves can be harvested for the dye pot but I prefer to wait until the flowering stalks develop and then harvest the whole flowering top. If the plants don't flower in their first season, they will usually flower the following year. The flowering spikes produce tiny black seeds inside little green pods and these can be shaken out and sown the following spring for the next crop. Weld also tends to self-seed readily. The tall stalks can be harvested for the dye pot when they are in flower, but leave one or two to produce seeds. The whole plant top is used in the dye pot and can be used fresh or dried. If used fresh, weld gives bright acidic yellows; dried weld sometimes gives less brilliant yellows. With an alum mordant, weld gives various shades of yellow. It can also be used without an alum mordant and colours almost as bright as those from an alum mordant can be achieved if an alkaline modifier is applied. Copper modifiers give a lime green, especially if an alkaline modifier has been used first, and iron modifiers give moss greens. The colour from weld can be extracted in several ways. One method is to pour boiling water over the dyestuff and leave it to steep overnight. The dye liquid can then be strained off and the fibres added and allowed to soak, without further application of heat, until they have developed a suitable depth of colour. This method works best with alum-mordanted fibres. The used weld dyestuff can then be processed again for a second dye bath, this time by the simmering method. The alkaline extraction method can also be used very successfully with weld (see page 32). Use 150% dyestuff for all methods.

Colours from dried weld
Left: Br.NM, Br.NM+A, Gr.NM, Gr.NM+A;
Centre from top: AM, NM, NM+A, NM+C, NM+A+C, NM+I, NM+A+I;
Right: tannin(W), tannin(B), tannin(B)+A, tannin(B)+C, tannin(B)+I

Colours from fresh weld
From left: AM+I, AM, AM+C

Colours from the alkaline
extraction method (NM)

Rhamnus spp. Buckthorn

Rhamnus cathartica

Berries from Rhamnus cathartica

Buckthorn has a long history as a dye plant and the berries of species of *Rhamnus* have been highly prized for centuries as a source of yellow dye. In addition to the berries, the leaves and bark of most species of buckthorn can also be used in the dye pot. The native British species is *Rhamnus cathartica*, which is a tall, spiny shrub found mainly on chalky ground in England, in hedgerows and on fens and scrub. It is one of only two food sources of the Brimstone butterfly, the other being alder buckthorn, *Frangula alnus* (see page 75). The berries of *Rhamnus cathartica* are a source of yellow dye and also fiercely purgative, hence its common name, purging buckthorn. The buckthorn berries generally sold as a dyestuff are usually the mature or immature berries of *Rhamnus infectorius*. This is an evergreen shrub, native to Italy, Spain, Southern France and parts of the Middle East. Buckthorn berries are also known to dyers as Persian berries, probably because those from Persia were considered superior. The dried, unripe berries were used as a yellow dye for centuries and were particularly useful for calico printing. The yellow component of the green in many old silks and calico prints came from Persian berries.

Rhamnus cathartica is such a valuable dye plant that it deserves a place in the dye garden, especially as a red dye can be extracted from the bark. With an alum mordant, buckthorn berries give clear yellows when green and immature; the ripe black berries give more mustard tones. If used without an alum mordant, the yellows are paler but they can be brightened with an alkaline modifier. Copper and iron modifiers give shades of green. Buckthorn leaves can be used fresh or dried but the fresh leaves give more intense colours. If used with an alum mordant, the leaves of buckthorn give colours very similar to those from the ripe berries. When used without an alum mordant, buckthorn leaves give browner shades; an alkaline modifier gives a rich brown, and copper and iron modifiers give shades of khaki. Buckthorn bark can be used without an alum mordant and, if the colour is extracted in the usual way, it gives shades of yellow and mustard; an alkaline modifier makes the colour pink-red, while iron and copper modifiers give a deep mustard tone. However, if buckthorn bark is processed using the alkaline extraction method, reds very similar to those from madder (*Rubia tinctorum*) can be achieved without an alum mordant (see page 32 for details of the alkaline extraction method). It is thought that in the Iron Age, in areas where madder and madder-related plants were not available, this method may have been used with buckthorn bark to produce red dyes. Use 150% dyestuff for leaves, and 75% to 100% for bark and berries.

Colours from buckthorn bark
Left: Br.NM, Gr.NM; Centre from top: NM, NM+A, NM+C, NM+I;
Right: tannin(W), tannin(B)

Colours from buckthorn leaves
Left: Br.NM+A, Gr.NM+A; Centre from top: AM, NM, NM+A, NM+C, NM+I;
Right: tannin(W), tannin(B)

Colours from unripe buckthorn berries
Left: Br.NM+A, Gr.NM+A; Centre from top: AM, NM, NM+A, NM+C, NM+I;
Right: tannin(B)

Colours from buckthorn bark alkaline extraction method
Left: Br.NM, Gr.NM; Right from the top: Reds becoming more orange in tone
as the dye bath decreases in strength & alkalinity (all NM & white wool)

Rheum spp. Rhubarb *

Young culinary rhubarb leaves

Dried rhubarb root

The roots of all species of rhubarb can be used in the dye pot and the leaves can be used both as a dye and as a mordant. Both the leaves and the root of rhubarb can be used successfully without an alum mordant. Rhubarb leaves give soft yellows but they contain poisonous oxalic acid and should be handled with care. Rhubarb root is a most versatile dye and provides shades of yellow, green, coral and pink. I usually use the roots of culinary rhubarb and, when the plants need to be divided, I harvest some roots for the dye pot and return the remaining roots to the ground. The roots can be used fresh or dried but when dry they can be difficult to chop up, so it is best to chop them up before drying them. They should be stored in paper bags in a dry place, as they tend to develop mould if they absorb moisture. The roots can also be kept in the freezer and this helps to break down the fibres and makes the roots easier to chop. For freezing, I usually pack the roots into plastic bags in quantities of about 50g (2oz) per bag, so I only need to defrost the amount of root I need each time. Make sure to label the bags very clearly and store them in the freezer in a cardboard box, also clearly labelled. Rhubarb root can be applied successfully without heat; with heat, it gives a clear yellow if the dye bath is kept below a simmer; simmering tends to give mustard yellows. If the colour is too mustard in tone, an acidic modifier will give a clearer yellow. An alkaline modifier gives shades of pink and even red if the alkaline solution is strong and the fibres are soaked in it for long enough. Copper modifiers give taupe/tan and iron modifiers give moss green. The alkaline extraction method can be used successfully with rhubarb root and produces shades of pink and red (see page 32 for details of this method). To remain pink, these colours must be dried away from the light. If they are dried in full sunlight, the colour changes to a grey-blue in a process known as photo-oxidisation. Use 75% to 100% dyestuff for rhubarb root and 200% for rhubarb leaves if used as a dye.

Colours from rhubarb root
Far left: Br.NM, Gr.NM;
Left from top: AM, NM, NM+A, NM+C, NM+I (dye bath simmered);
Centre: tannin(B); Right from top: NM, NM+A, NM+C, NM+I (gentle heat only)

Colours from a cool rhubarb root dye bath
Left to right: NM, NM+A, NM+C, NM+I

Colours from the alkaline extraction method
From top: NM, NM photo-oxidised, AM, AM photo-oxidised

Rubia peregrina Wild Madder

Wild madder

Rubia peregrina is an evergreen perennial which likes to grow through other vegetation. It has glossy green leaves and small yellow flowers, which can produce an abundance of seeds in good growing conditions. It is the native British form of madder and one of the sources of reds before the introduction into Britain of dyer's madder (*Rubia tinctorum*). Wild madder gives similar colours to those from dyer's madder and has been identified on textiles from the Anglo-Saxon period. *Rubia peregrina* can be grown from seed following the instructions given on page 117 for *Rubia tinctorum*, although seeds may be difficult to obtain unless collected from the wild. The roots are the parts used for dyeing and, as with other madder plants, they should not be harvested until the plants are at least three years old. The roots of wild madder can be used as described on page 118 for *Rubia tinctorum*. Use 200% dyestuff.

Colours from Rubia peregrina
Left: Br.NM, Gr.NM; Centre from top: AM, NM, NM+A, NM+C, NM+I;
Right: tannin(W), tannin(B)

Rubia tinctorum Dyer's Madder *

A flourishing madder bed

Harvested madder roots

Dyer's madder plants look like weeds. Their leafy tops feel rough and often sprawl untidily over the ground and their clusters of tiny yellow-green flowers are pale and insignificant. Yet to the dyer these rather uninteresting-looking plants are miracles of colour, because their roots contain alizarin, one of the most valuable red dye pigments ever known. Indeed, the synthesising of alizarin in 1869 was among the triumphs of early dyestuff chemistry.

Rubia tinctorum is native to the Middle East and the eastern parts of the Mediterranean. It is one of the most ancient dyes and was used by the early Egyptians and the Greeks and Romans. Madder was cultivated throughout Europe and the Middle East, but the finest quality was said to come from Turkey, Holland and France. Like several other dye plants, it was also used medicinally and Pliny mentioned that it was reported to cure jaundice. Madder was used to dye the red coats of British soldiers and reached the height of its fame as the dye used to produce the colour known as 'Turkey Red'.

Madder is easy to grow from seed, although it is a good idea to purchase one or two plants to start with, as the roots should not be harvested for at least three years after sowing the seeds. Madder prefers full sun but will tolerate some shade and is hardy to cold. It will grow in most well-drained, fertile garden soils, but the addition of some lime will encourage the roots to produce more dye pigment. Madder is not subject to diseases or pests and once established it requires very little care and attention. It may be advisable to wear gloves when handling madder plants, as they can cause a skin rash on some people. Seeds should be sown indoors in early spring several weeks before the last frost and the seedlings can be transplanted to their permanent positions when they are about 20 to 25cm (8 to 10in) high and look strong and healthy. Set the plants about 2ft (60cm) apart and keep the bed free of weeds, because madder can be propagated by layering. When the tops are about 45 to 60cm (18 to 24in) long, bend them down to the ground, gently because they break easily, and put some soil over them around the leaf joints. They will grow new roots from the joints and you can keep on doing this until you have a bed full of plants. In their second or third year, madder plants should flower and then produce green berries which turn black when mature. These contain one or two seeds and the berries can be collected and dried thoroughly, then stored and sown for more plants.

When the plants are three years old, you can start to harvest some roots. Dig a few plants up in the autumn, making sure to dig deeply enough to find all the roots. They are about the thickness of pencils and bright orange-red in colour. Wash the harvested roots well to remove not only the soil, but also some of the less desirable yellow and brown pigments which can dull the dye colours. Chop the madder roots up then spread them out on newspaper on a mesh tray or rack and dry them really thoroughly until they look brown and woody and have shrunk in size. Store them in a cool, dry place in paper sacks, never in plastic or polythene, as mould develops quite easily if they get damp. If they do become mouldy, you can still use them but the dye colour may be slightly duller. Madder roots can also be used fresh but chop them up or crush them well first, to obtain their maximum colour potential. The dried plant tops can also be used in the dye pot.

Madder is without question my favourite dye. It can be used successfully both with and without a mordant, it can be applied hot or cold and it will give a wide range of lovely shades, from orange and red to purple, pink and brown. It may not be the most beautiful of garden plants but the colour secrets hidden in its roots are truly amazing.

Dyeing with madder root

There are several ways of dyeing with madder root, which can be used successfully without an alum mordant, although an alum mordant may be necessary for deep, bright, true reds. Each method usually enables several successive batches of fibres to be dyed in the same solution and each batch of fibres will dye to a slightly different shade. Method A can also be used without heating the dye bath. Just put the madder root and fibres into a dye pot, fill the pot up with cold water and leave the fibres in the dye bath until a suitable depth of colour has been achieved. For each method use 100% madder roots and up to 150% if you want to be able to use several exhaust dye baths.

METHOD A

When I first started to use madder roots I followed this method, which is the one most commonly featured in dye books. Put the washed, chopped roots into the dye pot, together with the fibres to be dyed, add cold water and then gently heat the dye bath to just below simmering point. Maintain this level of heat, and no higher, for as long as necessary to achieve the desired depth of colour. At no point allow the dye bath to simmer. After the first batch of fibres has been removed, add further batches until the colour is exhausted. Each batch will dye to a paler shade as the dye potential of the dye bath decreases. With an alum mordant, this method gives shades of red and coral and if used without an alum mordant it tends to give orange or brownish colours. Alkaline modifiers make the colours pinker in tone, and iron and copper modifiers give shades of brown. In order to completely exhaust the dye potential, once the final fibres have been removed from the dye bath add 2–3 teaspoons of citric acid powder or 2 to 3 tablespoons of clear vinegar to the used dye bath including the madder pieces and simmer it for about 30 minutes to extract any remaining dye colour. Then strain off the dye solution, add some fibres and simmer them gently until all the dye has been used. This final dye bath usually gives orange shades. Nowadays, however, I tend to use the following Method B when dyeing with madder.

METHOD B

First of all wash the roots and then put them in a dye pot, pour boiling water over them, leave them to steep for about a minute and then strain off this liquid into a second dye pot. Repeat this process once more, adding the second strained-off solution to the first. This solution can be put to one side and used to make a dye bath later (see page 121). Then return to the roots and put them in a dye pot, fill up with water and simmer the roots for about 30 minutes. Allow the solution to cool for 5–10 minutes, then strain off the dye liquid and add the fibres to be dyed. Initially leave the fibres to steep in the dye bath for an hour or so without further heat and apply gentle heat only if you want the colour to deepen. However, once the fibres have been added, keep the dye bath well below a simmer.

Allow the fibres to cool in the dye bath, preferably overnight, before removing them and rinsing them well. The used roots can be simmered again to make a second dye bath for paler colours. Using modifiers will give results similar to those described for Method A.

The following three photos show 40 colours from one madder dye bath.

Colours from Method B (AM)
Left: Br., Br.+A,+C,+I, Gr., Gr.+A,+C,+I; Right from top: AM, CL, AM+A,+C,+I

Colours from Method B (NM, RL & tannin)
Left: Br.NM & Gr.NM; Centre: NM & RL; Right: tannin(W) & tannin(B)
All samples from top: No modifier, +A,+C,+I

Colours from the poured-off dye solution
From the top: NM x 2 (cold soak), AM (cold soak), NM (+heat)

Using the poured-off solution

The dye solution poured off when preparing the dye bath for Method B can be used as a dye bath with or without heat. Pour the dye solution into a dye pot and, if necessary, add more water to ensure the fibres can move freely in the dye bath. Don't add too many fibres initially and start by using the dye bath without applying heat. If unmordanted fibres are dyed first by soaking them for at least an hour in the cool dye liquid they often produce a lovely pink, while alum-mordanted fibres usually become coral. This dye bath can also be simmered, when it tends to give browner tones.

METHOD C The alkaline extraction method

This method is very successful with madder and by adding fibres at different stages a range of shades can be achieved from a single dye bath without any application of heat. It gives lovely pink colours on unmordanted fibres and on alum-mordanted fibres it tends to give colours that are redder in tone. First put the madder roots into a dye pot or a strong plastic container with a lid and fill it up with an alkaline solution. (The madder pieces can be put into a mesh bag or net if necessary, so they don't get tangled up in the fibres.) For the alkaline solution, I usually use either two to three parts wood ash water to one part water or 1–2 teaspoons of washing soda/soda ash per 500ml (1 pint) of water; the quantities don't need to be precise and the pH value should be about 10 to 11. More wood ash water or washing soda can be added if necessary to achieve pH10 or pH11 and there should be sufficient liquid to enable the fibres to move freely. Fibres (mordanted or unmordanted) can be added at this stage together with the madder pieces and allowed to steep in the solution for a day or two with no application of heat. Keep checking the colour as it develops and remove the fibres when you are satisfied with the colour. Fermentation will set in after a day or two and this will affect the colours achieved, so check the pH level each day and if necessary add more wood ash water or soda ash to maintain the alkalinity. I tend to leave unmordanted fibres to soak for two or three days, to enable a rich pink colour to develop before the solution loses its alkalinity; then I remove the fibres and allow the solution to ferment. Unmordanted fibres added to the fermenting dye bath will become shades of coral and orange, rather than pink. As time passes and the madder continues to ferment, the solution will become neutral or slightly acidic and the colours produced will become browner in tone. Once the solution is no longer alkaline, it can be simmered, together with the madder pieces, for about 45 minutes. Strain off the dye liquid and use it to make a dye bath as described above for Method B.

A range of colours from madder using the alkaline extraction method (NM & no heat applied)

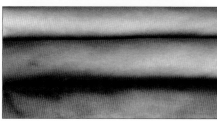

Some colours on silk from madder (NM and no heat applied)
From top: 2-day soak, 3-day soak, 4-day soak

METHOD D Aubergine purple from madder

First mordant the fibres using either iron water or a solution of ferrous sulphate. If you are using iron water as a mordant, dilute it at the rate of one part iron water to one part water. To make a ferrous sulphate solution, dissolve a ½ teaspoon of ferrous sulphate per 100g (4oz) fibres in hot water then add this to water in the pot. Add the wetted fibres, plus more water if necessary to ensure they can move freely in the liquid. Put a lid on the pot, bring slowly to simmering point and hold at this temperature for 30 minutes, moving the fibres around gently from time to time. Allow the solution to cool then remove the fibres and rinse them. Prepare the madder dye bath as described in Method B, add the fibres and simmer them gently for about 30 minutes. Leave them to cool then apply an alkaline modifier.

Aubergine purple from madder

METHOD E Madder root and crab apples

Crab apples can be added to madder dye baths to brighten the colour. This is particularly effective if an alum mordant has not been applied. I usually add one or two handfuls of chopped crab apples per 500g fibres. For Method A, simmer the crab apples first and then add this solution, plus the apples, to the madder dye bath. For Method B, simmer the crab apples together with the madder during the colour extraction process.

Colours from a madder dye bath with crab apples added
From top: AM, NM, tannin(B)

Dyeing with madder plant tops

Madder plant tops can also be used to make a dye bath. They usually give pink tones on alum-mordanted fibres and tan shades on unmordanted materials. Leave the plant tops until they dry out on the plants and look straw-like, then harvest them. They can be used immediately or dried and stored for use later. To make a dye bath, simmer the tops for 45 minutes to an hour, strain off the solution, add the fibres and simmer gently for about 45 minutes. Let the fibres cool in the dye bath before rinsing them. Use 150% to 200% plant tops.

Colours from madder plant tops
From top: AM, NM, NM+A

Rubus fruticosus Blackberry/Bramble

Blackberry leaves

Blackberry or bramble is a hardy, woody shrub, usually with thorns, which grows freely in the wild and is frequently cultivated for its fruits. When harvesting and processing blackberry, it is advisable to wear strong gloves to protect your hands from the thorns. The leafy shoots and stems of blackberry plants or brambles are rich in tannin and can be used as a tannin mordant (see page 29 for details). They can be used as a dye without an alum mordant and they produce shades of pale yellow and tan. An alum mordant gives a slightly brighter yellow. An alkaline modifier deepens the colour, a copper modifier gives an attractive green and an iron modifier gives grey. If iron water is added to the bramble dye solution this can give a deep grey dye if fibres are simmered in it for 30 to 45 minutes. Use 100% bramble shoots and tops if used as a tannin mordant and 200% if used as a dye.

Colours from bramble shoots and leaves
Left: Br.NM, Gr.NM; Centre from top: AM, NM, NM+A, NM+C, NM+I;
Right: tannin(W)

Rumex spp. Dock, Sorrel

Rumex obtusifolius leaves

Dried yellow dock root

There are several native British species of *Rumex*, including *Rumex crispus*, curled or yellow dock and *Rumex obtusifolius*, broad-leaved dock. The leaves, roots and mature dried seeds of all types of *Rumex* can be used in the dye pot. Dock roots contain tannins that act as natural mordants and the roots of *Rumex crispus* and *Rumex obtusifolius* also contain iron, so dock roots can be used as a mordant or base for other dyes. All parts of dock can be used without an alum mordant. Dock roots give yellow, brown and orange colours and the leaves give tans and yellows. To extract the dye colour from the roots, soak them in water overnight then simmer them for about an hour. Mature stems of dock with dried seeds can sometimes give coral and even red colours on alum-mordanted wool if they are harvested at the end of summer but before November, especially after a very dry, hot summer. To make the dye bath, the seeds should be simmered for several hours or until the liquid is deep red in colour. Use 100% dyestuff for the roots and 150% for leaves and seeds.

Colours from yellow dock root
Left: Br.NM, Gr.NM; Centre from top: AM, NM, NM+A, NM+C, NM+I;
Right: tannin(W), tannin(B)

125

Salix spp. Willow

Leaves of white willow (Salix alba)   *Bark of goat willow (Salix caprea)*

The bark and leaves of all species of willow can be used for dyeing and willow bark can also be used as a mordant (see page 29). Willow leaves usually give yellows with an alum mordant; without an alum mordant they give tan and brown colours. On unmordanted fibres, the fresh leaves of white willow (*Salix alba*) give shades of tan and brown; with an alum mordant fresh leaves can give rich rust colours. The colours from willow bark usually range from pinkish tan to rust, depending on the species and the extraction method used; an alkaline modifier can enhance these colours and iron and copper modifiers make the colours browner. With the alkaline colour extraction method white willow bark gives soft pink colours. Use 200% dyestuff for leaves and bark.

Colours from the leaves of goat willow (Salix caprea)
Left: Br.NM, Gr.NM; Centre from top: AM, NM, NM+A, NM+C, NM+I;
Right: tannin(W), tannin(B)

Colours from the leaves of white willow (Salix alba)
Left: Br.NM, Gr.NM; Centre from top: AM, NM, NM+A, NM+C, NM+I;
Right: tannin(W), tannin(B)

Colours from the bark of white willow (Salix alba)
Left: Br.NM, Gr.NM; Centre from top: AM, NM, NM+A, NM+C, NM+I;
Right: tannin(W), tannin(B)

Salvia officinalis Sage

Sage in flower

Sage is a perennial culinary herb, which also features as a dye plant in some dye recipes from the Middle Ages. It was mentioned in the first known manual written for the professional dyer, the *Plictho de larte de tentori*, an important collection of recipes for dyeing wool, silk, cotton and linen, compiled by Gioanventura Rosetti, Master of the Arsenal in Venice, and published in Venice in 1548. Sage is a useful source of muted greenish-yellow colours, especially if used with an alum mordant. Sage leaves and tops, with or without the flowers, can be harvested at any time of the year and I have found the dye pot an excellent way of using the flowered tops from my sage bushes, which need regular pruning. If used without an alum mordant, sage tops give soft creamy-tan colours. An alkaline modifier intensifies the colours and copper and iron modifiers give various shades of mossy green. Use 200% dyestuff.

Colours from sage leaves and plant tops
Left: Br.NM, Gr.NM; Centre from top: AM, NM, NM+A, NM+C, NM+I;
Right: tannin(B)

Sambucus spp. Elder

Sambucus nigra in spring

The bark and leaves of all species of elder can be used in the dye pot. Elderberries can also be used as a dyestuff but the colours they give do not have good light-fastness and for that reason I do not wholeheartedly recommend them. However, for dyers who are not too concerned with the permanence of the colours they achieve, fresh elderberries give attractive purples if used with an alum mordant. Dried elderberries usually give shades of brown. Elder leaves give a creamy colour if used without an alum mordant; an alkaline modifier deepens this colour and iron or copper modifiers give delicate shades of green. If used with an alum mordant, elder leaves give yellows. Elder bark gives creamy beige colours and an iron modifier produces soft shades of grey. Use 150% to 200% dyestuff for both leaves and bark.

Colours from leaves of Sambucus nigra
Left: Br.NM+A, Gr.NM+A; Centre from top: AM, NM, NM+A, NM+C, NM+I;
Right: tannin(W)+A, tannin(B)+A

Serratula tinctoria Saw-wort

Saw-wort leaves in spring

Saw-wort in flower

Saw-wort is a perennial wild plant with purple thistle-like flowers and serrated-edged leaves and it is sometimes available from companies specialising in wild plants. Its main dye component is luteolin and it produces colours similar to those from weld (*Reseda luteola*). Saw-wort has a long history as a dye plant. It was widely used in Europe in the Middle Ages, especially in areas where weld was not harvested, and in Tuscany during the fourteenth and fifteenth centuries it was as highly regarded as weld. The whole plant top is used for dyeing and gives deep yellows with an alum mordant; without an alum mordant the yellows are pale unless an alkaline modifier is applied. Iron and copper modifiers give soft greens. Use 100% to 150% dyestuff.

Colours from saw-wort plant tops
Left: Br.NM+A, Gr.NM+A; Centre from top: AM, CL, RL, NM, NM+A, NM+C, NM+I;
Right: tannin(B)

Solidago spp. Goldenrod

Solidago canadensis

Goldenrod is a perennial plant that makes an attractive addition to the garden and all species of goldenrod can be used in the dye pot. The native British species of goldenrod is *Solidago virgaurea*. However, the species most frequently planted in gardens is *Solidago canadensis*, native to North America but which has become naturalised in Britain and can often be found growing on wasteland. With an alum mordant, the plant tops of goldenrod give lovely bright yellow colours; without an alum mordant they give cream to pale yellow shades, which become soft greens with alkaline, copper and iron modifiers. The shades of yellow obtained with an alum mordant vary according to whether the whole plant tops or just the flower heads are used. The flower heads used alone produce brighter clearer yellows, especially if the dye bath is kept below a simmer. Use 150% to 200% flowers or plant tops.

Colours from goldenrod plant tops
Left: Br.NM, Gr.NM; Centre from top: AM, NM, NM+A, NM+C, NM+I;
Right: tannin(W), tannin(B)

Tanacetum parthenium Feverfew

Feverfew

Feverfew is a perennial plant with scented leaves and daisy-like flowers. It is traditionally used in herbal medicines, mainly to reduce fever and to treat headaches. Feverfew makes a very attractive garden plant and can sometimes be found in the wild. Plants can often be purchased from garden centres but feverfew can also be grown from seed. Sow the seeds in spring and plant the seedlings out as soon as all danger of frost has passed. If started early enough, the plants should flower in their first year. The whole flowering top, either fresh or dried, can be used in the dye pot and I usually wait until the flowers have faded, then cut the plants back and use the prunings in the dye pot. Feverfew gives a strong yellow with an alum mordant; if used without an alum mordant it gives paler yellows. An alkaline modifier used on grey and brown fibres dyed in feverfew gives rich moss greens, and iron and copper modifiers give attractive soft green shades. Use 150% to 200% dyestuff.

Colours from feverfew plant tops
Left: Br.NM+A, Gr.NM+A; Centre from top: AM, NM, NM+A, NM+C, NM+I;
Right: tannin(B)

Tanacetum vulgare Tansy

Tansy

Tansy is a strongly aromatic perennial plant, which spreads by underground runners. It can frequently be found growing in the wild on grassland and waste ground. The leaves are bright green and deeply serrated and the leafy stems bear clusters of flat button-like golden yellow flowers throughout the summer and well into the autumn. Tansy can be grown from seed and tolerates most conditions but it can be very invasive. The whole plant tops or just the flower heads can be used in the dye bath and should be harvested when the plant is in flower from summer to autumn. They can be used fresh or dried. If tansy plant tops are used without an alum mordant they give soft greenish yellow colours, which become various shades of mossy green if modifiers are applied. Tansy gives yellow colours with an alum mordant and these yellows are clearer if only the flower heads are used. Use 150% dyestuff.

Colours from tansy plant tops
Left: Br.NM+A, Gr.NM+A; Centre from top: AM, NM, NM+A, NM+C, NM+I;
Right: tannin(B)

Taxus baccata Yew

Yew leaves

Yew wood shavings

Yew trees are often found in churchyards and many are hundreds of years old. Yew heartwood can produce rust shades and it may be possible to obtain wood shavings from a wood-turner. Otherwise yew shavings or chips can be purchased from some suppliers of dyestuffs. With an alum mordant, yew shavings give rusty orange colours but these are duller without an alum mordant; alkaline modifiers make the colour browner, copper modifiers give warm tans and iron modifiers give greys. The leafy twigs of yew give yellows, tans and browns. Use 100% dyestuff for wood shavings and 200% for leaves.

Colours from yew wood shavings (above) and leafy twigs (below)
Left: Br.NM+A, Gr.NM+A; Centre from top: AM, NM, NM+A, NM+C, NM+I;
Right: tannin(W), tannin(B)

Tilia cordata Lime

Lime leaves in spring

Lime trees, also called linden trees, can sometimes live for several hundred years and are often grown as ornamental specimens. Bees love the small scented flowers and the white, finely grained wood of the lime tree is valued for carving. Lime is not frequently mentioned as a source of dye colour but there are several magnificent lime trees near my house and it seemed a good opportunity to experiment with lime leaves in the dye pot. To make the dye bath, first pour boiling water over the leaves and leave them to soak overnight, then simmer the leaves for about an hour to extract the dye colour. Lime leaves produce useful, if unremarkable, colours. If used with an alum mordant they give delicate yellows and without an alum mordant they give pale tan colours. An alkaline modifier gives a soft red-brown and iron and copper modifiers give soft shades of green. Use 150% to 200% dyestuff.

Colours from lime leaves
Left: Br.NM, Gr.NM; Centre from top: AM, NM, NM+A, NM+C, NM+I;
Right: tannin(B)

Using Lichens for Dyeing

Lichens are remarkable organisms composed of fungal and algal partners growing together in a symbiotic relationship. Most lichens are slow-growing and should not be gathered indiscriminately for dyeing. Also, many species are protected and it is against the law to collect these from the wild. Lichens can sometimes be found lying on the ground after high winds or growing on felled branches awaiting the chainsaw and it is acceptable to harvest them under these circumstances. Otherwise, unless they are growing in great abundance or in situations where they would be destroyed anyway, lichens should not be collected for the dye pot, except for very small-scale test purposes.

If simmered to make a dye bath, most lichens give yellow, brown and rust colours but as these colours can be obtained from other sources there is generally no need to use lichens to achieve them. However, the purple colours available from a few species of lichen are beautiful rich, vivid shades of historical importance and for this reason lichens are included in this book.

Purple is not a colour which can be obtained from many sources. In the Graeco-Roman world, the extremely costly Tyrian or Imperial Purple dye from shellfish became the symbol of luxurious living and was reserved for the elite. The Romans used the lichen *Roccella tinctoria* to produce a similar but less costly purple dye. In Britain this purple colour was obtained mainly from the lichens *Ochrolechia tartarea* and *Umbilicaria pustulata* and lichen purple has been identified on early textile fragments from several areas of Europe.

Very few species of lichen will give purple dyes, so it is important to make sure you have correctly identified the appropriate lichen. One way of testing for the presence of purple dye is to scratch the surface of the lichen with a pin or the point of a knife and then put a few drops of household bleach on to the scratched area. If the lichen shows a red or purple colour, it should give a purple dye. No mordant is required for dyes from lichens and about 10% dyestuff is required for lichen purple; for test purposes, a piece of lichen about 5cm (2in) square should yield enough purple dye for a small sample. For my tests I used the lichen *Ochrolechia tartarea*.

To extract and use the purple colour, first crumble up the lichen and put it into a strong glass jar with a well-fitting lid. Make a solution of one part water to one part household ammonia (stale urine was used in the past) and add this to the jar until the lichen is well covered and the jar is half to three-quarters full. Stir very well then put the lid on firmly. Shake or stir the mixture several times every day. After a few weeks the solution should be a rich purple colour and is ready to use. Strain off the liquid into a dye pot, top up with water and add the fibres to be dyed. Heat the solution gradually to simmering point and simmer gently for about 45 minutes then remove from the heat. Leave the fibres in the solution for 24 hours then remove them and squeeze the excess liquid back into the pot. Rinse the dyed fibres and store them away from the light. Any remaining dye solution can be re-used until exhausted.

NB: Handle ammonia with care, work in a well-ventilated area and don't inhale any fumes.

Lichen Ochrolechia tartarea

Lichen soaking in ammonia/water

Shades of lichen purple from Ochrolechia tartarea on white wool (NM)

If clear vinegar is added to a lichen purple dye bath, it will make the colours redder in tone. Add the vinegar gradually a teaspoon at a time until the dye bath becomes a rich red but be careful not to add too much vinegar.

Left: Colours from a lichen purple dye bath to which clear vinegar has been added Right: Lichen purple exhaust on (from top) white wool, brown wool & grey wool (NM)

A few lichens, for example *Evernia prunastri*, give yellows, rusts and browns if simmered to extract the dye colour and a brownish purple if used as described above for purple from *Ochrolechia tartarea*. Also, the relatively common orange-coloured lichen, *Xanthoria parietina*, which grows widely on rooftops and walls, will give pink and blue-grey colours if treated in the same way as the traditional purple-producing lichens, such as *Ochrolechia tartarea*. Some householders find this orange lichen undesirable and scrape it off their walls and rooftops so, if you are in the right place at the right time, it may be possible to obtain samples for the dye pot.

Lichen Evernia prunastri   *Lichen Xanthoria parietina*

Xanthoria parietina gives shades of soft pink, rather than purple and, once the fibres have been dyed, they should be dried in a dark place away from the light. If the fibres are dried in the sunlight, they photo-oxidise to a soft grey-blue so, by drying one set of fibres away from the light and a second set in direct sunlight, two colours can be obtained from the same dye bath.

Colours from Xanthoria parietina
From the top: pale yellow fibres from the simmering method, pink fibres dried away
from the light, blue-grey fibres dried in the sunlight (all NM)

Using Fungi for Dyeing

There is some evidence from recipes in dyers' handbooks from the fifteenth century that certain types of fungi may have been used by dyers during the later Middle Ages, mainly as an ingredient in dyeing various shades of crimson with the insect dye kermes. However, fungi do not seem to have been widely used traditionally for dyeing in the past and their increasing popularity among craft dyers seems to be a relatively recent phenomenon.

Some colours from fungi

The range of colours available from fungi is remarkable and those people fortunate enough to live in areas where fungi are abundant may be able to achieve colours ranging from brown and yellow to red and purple, if they can find the appropriate species. It is important to be aware that many fungi are poisonous, so great care should be exercised when harvesting mushrooms and other fungi for the dye pot. Also, some fungi may be protected species, so always check before collecting any for dyeing.

In my experience, the majority of fungi found locally to me tend to give shades of brown and yellow. However, some *Cortinarius* species of mushrooms contain some of the same dye pigments as madder and give very similar colours. In general, fungi are used in the dye pot following the methods used for the majority of other dyes and react in similar ways to colour modifiers. Although many fungi can be used without an alum mordant, brighter clearer colours are often obtained on alum-mordanted materials and I would recommend using both unmordanted and alum-mordanted fibres if you are testing fungi for the first time. Use between 50% and 100% dyestuff.

The photos below show some of the colours available from the following fungi: *Cortinarius spp.*, *Hapalopilus nidulans*, *Hydnellum aurantiacum*, *Phaeolus schweinitzii*, *Pisolithius tinctorius*, *Tapinella atrotomentosa*.

All the samples are wool; samples labelled A are on unmordanted fibres and samples labelled B have been mordanted with alum. The number 1 = no modifier, the number 2 = alkaline modifier and the number 3 = iron modifier. Other samples are from exhaust dye baths, some plus modifiers.

Colours from mixed Cortinarius spp. on unmordanted wool

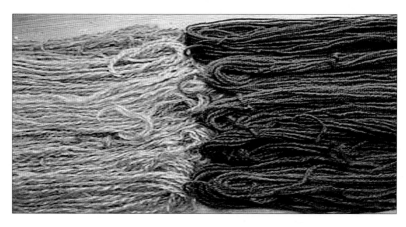

Colours from Cortinarius semisanguineus
Left from top: NM, NM+A, NM exhaust, NM+A, NM+C, NM+I;
Right from top: AM, AM exhaust, AM+A, AM+C, AM+I

Cortinarius semisanguineus in the wild (left) and harvested for dyeing (right)

Colours from Hydnellum aurantiacum (left) and Tapinella atrotomentosa (right)

Hydnellum aurantiacum   *Tapinella atrotomentosa*

Colours from mixed Cortinarius spp.

Colours from Cortinarius sanguineus

Colours from Phaeolus schweinitzii

Cortinarius sanguineus

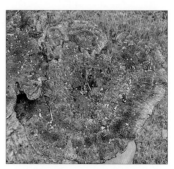

Phaeolus schweinitzii

143

Colours from Pisolithius tinctorius

Left: Hapalopilus nidulans (Syn. H. rutilans)
Right: Purples from Hapalopilus nidulans (Top skein: alum mordant and lower skein no mordant)

Bracket fungi can be used in the same way as other dyes. However, at least from my experience of using bracket fungi found locally, most give predominantly brown, yellow and tan colours. Deeper shades are achieved with an alum mordant but most bracket fungi can also be used without an alum mordant. However, as they generally tend to give colours readily available from other sources, and look so attractive when growing in the wild, I prefer not to harvest bracket fungi for the dye pot.

Bracket fungus growing at the base of a tree

Bracket fungus on a tree trunk

A Brief Outline of Some of the Dyes used in Europe from the Iron Age to the Middle Ages

The Iron Age (800 BCE–43 CE)

Although very few textile fragments or textile-related artefacts from this period are available for technical analysis, there is some evidence to indicate that the dyes used during this period in northern Europe included woad (*Isatis tinctoria*) for blues, and weld (*Reseda luteola*) and dyer's broom (*Genista tinctoria*) for yellows. Birch leaves (*Betula spp.*), heather (*Calluna vulgaris*), saw-wort (*Serratula tinctoria*), chamomile (*Chamaemelum nobile*), and possibly other native plants, were probably also used for yellow and gold colours. Bedstraws, such as lady's bedstraw (*Galium verum*) and hedge bedstraw (*Galium mollugo*), and wild madder (*Rubia peregrina*) were the most likely sources of red and coral colours, and buckthorn bark (*Rhamnus spp.*) may also have been used for reds. Tannins from sources such as tree barks, alder, oak and other native trees were used, sometimes in combination with other dyes. Some species of lichen, for example *Ochrolechia spp.* and *Umbilicaria spp.* were used for purples.

There is some evidence from the Hallstatt textiles of imported dyes, such as the insect dyes kermes (*Kermes vermilio*) and Polish or Armenian cochineal (*Porphyrophora polonica*), although it may have been the materials showing traces of these dyes that were imported, rather than the dyestuffs themselves. It is not known whether mineral alum would have been readily available as a mordant in the Iron Age, although it is not impossible, but iron and copper could have been available in the form of iron and copper waters (see page 36) or from iron and copper pots used as dye vessels.

Further information on Iron Age dyes can be found on pages 10–12.

The Romans (Romans in Britain 43 CE–410 CE)

According to Pliny the Elder, orange, red and purple were colours worn by priests and priestesses. Purple was the colour for high officials and the clothing of Emperors was dyed purple using a dye from shellfish of the *Murex* and *Purpura* genera. This mollusc dye, known as Tyrian or Imperial Purple, was very expensive and vast quantities of shellfish were required to produce relatively small amounts of dye matter. A less costly purple dye from the lichen *Roccella tinctoria* was used to simulate the purple from shellfish. Woad (*Isatis tinctoria*) was used by the Romans as a source of indigo blue dye. The insect dye kermes (*Kermes vermilio*) was used for reds. Madder (*Rubia tinctorum*) was also a source of red dye and, according to Pliny, it was cultivated near Rome around 50 CE. The yellow from weld (*Reseda luteola*) was the colour worn by the six Vestal Virgins and was also the colour of wedding garments. Oak galls were used by the Romans in combination with iron to make a black dye.

According to Pliny, a solution made from the outer green hulls of walnuts (*Juglans spp.*) was used as a brown dye for wool and also for hair. Pliny also states that saffron (*Crocus sativus*) was cultivated in Abruzzo and Sicily and was used as a yellow dye. Yellow was also obtained from the roots of turmeric (*Curcuma longa*), which was imported from the Orient during Imperial times.

It is interesting to note that, although the Romans would have used madder when they were in Britain, its use in Britain appears to have ceased for a period after their departure around 410 CE. This would seem to suggest that the Romans imported madder from Rome as a prepared dried dyestuff, rather than cultivating it in Britain.

The Romans used alum as a mordant and also iron but, as was probably the case with madder, it is likely that alum was imported into Britain from Italy for Roman use and ceased to be available in Britain after the Romans left, until it was imported later in the Anglo-Saxon period.

The Anglo-Saxons (410 CE–1066 CE)
The Anglo-Scandinavian Viking Period (c. 850 CE–1066 CE)

From the evidence available, the Anglo-Saxons seem to have used a limited number of dyes and those they did use were mainly the classic traditional dyes still favoured by British dyers today – for example, madder and madder-related plants for reds; indigo from woad (*Isatis tinctoria*) for blues; and weld (*Reseda luteola*) and dyer's broom (*Genista tinctoria*) for yellows. As outlined above, madder (*Rubia tinctorum*) would have been used in Britain by the Romans, but it seems to have disappeared from use for a period of time following their departure around 410 CE. This would seem to suggest that madder was imported by the Romans as a dried dyestuff, rather than being cultivated in Britain. In the early Anglo-Saxon period, dyers relied on native sources of red and coral colours, which were provided by madder-related plants, such as wild madder (*Rubia peregrina*), hedge bedstraw (*Galium mollugo*) and lady's bedstraw (*Galium verum*). There is evidence that madder (*Rubia tinctorum*) was in use later in the period and there is some indication that it was traded from France in the seventh and eighth centuries. In the later Anglo-Saxon period madder was cultivated in Britain and its use became widespread.

Other dyes used by the Anglo-Saxons include tannin-rich dyes for tan and brown shades and also for dark grey and black, when used with iron. Tannins are present in many plants and in oak galls, acorns, nuts and barks. However, it is not possible to identify by dye analysis the precise source of tannin in excavated fragments. For my Anglo-Saxon dye experiments I used both oak galls and bramble leaves and twigs as tannin mordants. I also used alder leaves and twigs, oak leaves and acorns to dye browns, and black with the addition of iron. Clearly there would have been an abundance of tannin-rich materials available in the countryside, so these shades would have been easy to produce. Another tannin-rich dye plant is walnut (*Juglans spp.*), which is not native but was possibly introduced by the Romans and was certainly growing here by 1000 CE. For purples there is some evidence that lichens of the species *Ochrolechia* and *Umbilicaria* were used and when treated in stale urine, which contains ammonia, these lichens can give purples and reds of considerable beauty and brilliance, although their light-fastness is limited. However, purple-producing lichens are found mainly in northern and western Britain, on rocky coastlines or in hilly areas, so the fact that they do not appear to have been widely used may reflect their scarcity in many areas of Anglo-Saxon England. As far as mordants are concerned, there is some doubt as to whether Mediterranean mineral alum would have been readily available to the early Anglo-Saxons. Although the Romans would have probably brought alum for their own use, it is likely that, as with madder, it disappeared with them when they left Britain. So the Anglo-Saxons may have had to rely on alternatives until imported alum was more widely available later in the period. Even then, I suspect that dyers working in a simple domestic environment would have relied solely on what they could grow and gather locally. Some plants, notably clubmosses, have the ability to absorb aluminium from the ground in which they grow, so it is possible that the Anglo-Saxons may have extracted aluminium from these plants. There is evidence from the Viking age site in York that clubmoss was used there, probably as a mordant, but the species of clubmoss found was unknown in Britain at that time, so it is likely that it was brought by the Vikings specifically for use as a mordant. It is also possible that tannin from plants may have been used as a fixative. Iron would probably also have been used, possibly in the form of iron water or by adding scraps of iron to the dye pot. If iron pots were used as dye vessels, this may also have had an effect on the colours.

Typical Anglo-Saxon colours from madder, oak bark, weld and woad

Some Anglo-Saxon dye colours from my experiments

The Mediaeval Period (1066 CE–1500 CE)

The dyes used in the later Anglo-Saxon and the Viking period, for example woad (*Isatis tinctoria*), madder (*Rubia tinctorum*), weld (*Reseda luteola*) and dyer's broom (*Genista tinctoria*), continued in use and gradually more dyes were introduced from other countries as trade developed. The Tyrian Purple dye industry had become considerably reduced by the Middle Ages and with the fall of Constantinople in 1453 it more or less disappeared. Kermes (*Kermes vermilio*), a valuable insect dye from shield-lice living on the kermes oak found in various parts of the Mediterranean, was an important item of trade and the most expensive of dyestuffs. Kermes became just as important as Tyrian Purple had been in the ancient world but today it is very difficult to obtain, although it was available from Algeria for a time in the late twentieth century and it may still occasionally be found on host trees around the Mediterranean.

Kermes (Kermes vermilio)

Wool dyed with kermes (AM)

A range of shades from kermes
From top: AM+A, AM (2 skeins), AM + citric acid modifier

Yellow dyes included the rind of the pomegranate (*Punica granatum*), young fustic from the stems and branches of Venetian sumac (*Cotinus coggygria*) and saffron (*Crocus sativus*), which became a valuable trade commodity. Dyes introduced in the late Middle Ages included sanderswood (*Pterocarpus santalinus*) from India and Ceylon and used for reddish rusts and compound colours, and sappanwood (*Caesalpinia sappan*) from Malaysia, which produced reds similar to those from brazilwood (*Caesalpinia echinata*), which was not imported into Europe until the beginning of the sixteenth century, following the discovery of the sea route to the Americas. Mediterranean alum also became more readily available and was imported into Britain from Italy, Spain and Asia Minor. Italy dominated trade and Italian dyers had access to dyes that were not generally available in many other parts of Europe. The fourteenth century archives of Francesco di Datini in Florence and Prato list lac (*Kerria lacca*), an insect dye from India and South-east Asia, and indigo (*Indigofera tinctoria*) from Baghdad among their items of trade. Dyeing flourished in Europe during the mediaeval period; guilds of master dyers became established and a master dyer's recipe book was closely guarded. Indeed, during the Middle Ages it was the craft of the dyer that added most to the value of textile fabrics. The list of dyes and details of dyeing techniques found in dyers' recipe books of the period indicate the increased complexity of some of the methods. There were also apparently regional differences in the use of colour. Flanders was known for green, the Rhineland for black and Britain for red. Within England, some towns were licensed during the mediaeval period to produce certain colours – for example, York for red and purple, Lincoln for green, scarlet and grey, Coventry for blue and Beverley for blue and red.

The Post-Mediaeval Period

Following the discovery in the late fifteenth century of the sea routes to the East Indies and the Americas, other significant dyes were introduced into Europe in the sixteenth century. One of the most important of these was indigo (*Indigofera tinctoria*) from the East for blues. Other dyes to arrive in Europe at this time from Southern and Central America included logwood (*Haematoxylon campechianum*) for purples, brazilwood (*Caesalpinia echinata*) for reds, the insect dye cochineal (*Dactylopius coccus*) for pinks and reds, and fustic (*Chlorophora tinctoria* or *Morus tinctoria*) for yellows. All these new dyes rapidly became valuable items of trade.

Dried cochineal insects

Pinks from cochineal (AM)

The shade of red for which cochineal probably became most famous is a brilliant scarlet, the colour of English huntsmen's jackets. This colour was found, possibly by accident, in the early seventeenth century by a Dutch engineer and alchemist, Cornelius Drebbel, who discovered that the addition of tin to cochineal resulted in a brilliant red colour. Once dyers had mastered the use of tin in cochineal dyeing, this red colour was much in demand. It was used for the uniforms of British army officers and Gloucestershire became famous for scarlet woollens dyed with cochineal and tin.

Drebbel's Scarlet from cochineal

Purple from logwood (Haematoxylon campechianum) (AM)

Indigo plants (Indigofera spp.)

Reds from Caesalpinia echinata (AM)

Health and Safety Guidelines

- Store all dyes, mordants, assistants and modifiers in clearly labelled containers and keep them well away from children, pets and food.
- Handle all substances with care, as some mordants and dyestuffs are poisonous or irritant. Take particular care with the following:
  - o Aluminium: irritant, harmful if ingested
  - o Iron: harmful if ingested
  - o Copper: poisonous
  - o Rhubarb leaves: poisonous
  - o Washing soda/soda ash: irritant, harmful if ingested
  - o Calcium hydroxide (slaked lime): irritant, harmful if ingested.
- Never add water to the reducing agents used in woad/indigo dyeing; they generate heat when wet and could catch fire. Always add them slowly to water.
- Slaked lime (calcium hydroxide) can irritate skin and lungs and cause serious injury if it comes into contact with the eyes. Do not pour water on to it but add it slowly to water.
- Do not eat, drink, handle food or smoke when carrying out any of the processes involved in mordanting and dyeing.
- Reserve pots, containers, strainers and all other equipment especially for mordanting and dyeing, and make sure they are labelled. Never use the same pots and equipment for food preparation or storage.
- Put a lid on the pots when in use to avoid inhaling any steam or fumes.
- Wear rubber gloves, an apron, and a dust-mask if you are asthmatic.
- Use oven gloves when handling hot equipment.
- Always work in a well-ventilated area.
- If you work in the kitchen, never prepare or handle food at the same time. Make sure all spills are mopped up immediately and wash work surfaces well after use. Avoid using any poisonous substances if working in the kitchen.
- All fine powders, whether toxic or non-toxic, are potentially harmful if inhaled, so wear a dust-mask when using powdered substances.
- Seek medical advice if any substances come into contact with eyes.
- Never pour anything away near where children or pets play, into wells or near a septic tank.
- Dilute all solutions containing residues of mordants or modifiers with plenty of water before disposal. These diluted solutions can then be poured down the drain or on the ground in an isolated spot.
- Most used plant materials can be put in the compost bin and most used dye baths can be poured down the drain or on the ground.
- Before disposing of indigo or woad vats, use up any remaining reducing agent by whisking them well to introduce oxygen.

Bibliography

Adrosko, R.J., *Natural Dyes and Home Dyeing*, New York, USA, Dover Publications, 1971.

Balfour-Paul, J., *Indigo*, London, England, British Museum Press, 1998.

Bichler, P., Gromer, K., Hofmann-de Keijzer, R., Kern, A., and Reschreiter, H. (eds.), *Hallstatt Textiles: Technical Analysis, Scientific Investigation*, Oxford, England, Archaeopress, 2005.

Böhmer, H., *Koekboya*, Ganderkesee, Germany, REMHÖB-Verlag, 2002.

Brunello, F. *The Art of Dyeing in the History of Mankind*, trans. B. Hickey, Vicenza, Italy, Neri Pozza, 1973 (made available by Phoenix Dye Works, Cleveland, Ohio, USA).

Buchanan, R., *A Dyer's Garden*, Loveland, Colorado, USA, Interweave Press, 1995.

Buchanan, R., *A Weaver's Garden*, Loveland, Colorado, USA, Interweave Press, 1987.

Cardon, D., *Natural Dyes*, London, England, Archetype Publications, 2007.

Casselman, K., *Craft of the Dyer*, Revised 2nd edition, New York, USA, Dover Publications, 1993.

Casselman, K., *Lichen Dyes: The New Source Book*, New York, USA, Dover Publications, 2001.

Chenciner, R., *Madder Red*, Richmond, England, Curzon Press, 2000.

Dalby, G., *Natural Dyes, Fast or Fugitive*, Somerset, England, Ashill Publications, 1985.

Dalby, G., *Natural Dyes for Vegetable Fibres*, Somerset, England, Ashill Publications, 1992.

Dean, J., *Colours from Nature*, Kent, England, Search Press, 2009.

Dean, J., *The Craft of Natural Dyeing*, Kent, England, Search Press, 1994.

Dean, J., *Wild Colour*, Revised 2nd edition, London, England and New York, USA, Mitchell Beazley and Watson-Guptill, 2010.

Delamare, F., and Guineau, B., *Colour: Making and Using Dyes and Pigments*, London, England, Thames & Hudson, 2000.

Fieler, G., *Farben aus der Natur*, Hannover, Germany, Verlag M & H Schaper, 1981.

Flint, I., *Eco Colour*, Sydney, Australia, Murdoch Books, 2008.

Flint, I., *Second Skin*, Sydney, Australia, Murdoch Books, 2011.

Goodwin, J., *A Dyer's Manual*, 2nd edition, England, Ashmans Publications, 2003.

Grae, I., *Nature's Colors*, Oregon, USA, Robin & Russ, 1991.

Grierson, S., *The Colour Cauldron*, Perth, Scotland, Mill Books, 1986.

Hofenk de Graaff, J., *The Colourful Past*, London, England, Archetype Publications, 2004.

Hummel, J. J., *The Dyeing of Textile Fabrics*, London, England, Cassell & Company, 1888.

Kendall, T., and Lambert, E., *The Complete Guide to Natural Dyeing*, Kent, England, Search Press, 2010.

Liles, J. N., *The Art and Craft of Natural Dyeing*, USA, University of Tennessee Press, 1990.

Ponting, K. G., *A Dictionary of Dyes and Dyeing*, London, England, Bell & Hyman Ltd., 1981.

Rhind, W., *A History of the Vegetable Kingdom*, London, England, Blackie & Son, 1865.

Rice, M., *Mushrooms for Dyes, Paper, Pigments and Myco-Stix*, USA, Mushrooms for Colour Press, 2007.

Roquero, A., *Tintes y tintereros de America*, Madrid, Spain, Ministry of Culture, 2006.

Sandberg, G., *Indigo Textiles*, London, England and Asheville, USA, A & C. Black and Lark Books, 1989.

Sandberg, G., *The Red Dyes*, Asheville, USA, Lark Books, 1997.

Schweppe, H., *Handbuch der Naturfarbstoffe*, Germany, ecomed Verlagsgesellschaft, 1993.

Walton Rogers, P., *Cloth and Clothing in Early Anglo-Saxon England*, York, England, Council for British Archaeology, 2007.

Walton Rogers, P., *Textile Production at 16-22 Coppergate*, York, England, Council for British Archaeology, 1997.

DVD

Colours of Provence using Sustainable Methods – Natural Dye Workshop with Michel Garcia, USA, Slow Fibre Studios, 2011, (DVD).

Suppliers

Dyes, Mordants, Yarns and Fibres

D T Craft and Design, 7 Fonthill Grove, Sale, Cheshire, UK, M33 4FR www.dtcrafts.co.uk

Garthenor Organic Pure Wool, Llanio Road, Tregaron, Wales, UK, SY25 6UR
www.organicpurewool.co.uk

Helen Melvin, Fiery Felts
Blaen Wern, The Waen, Bodfari, Denbighshire, Wales, UK, LL16 4BT
www.fieryfelts.co.uk

The Honorwood Flocks
Peter & Christine Everitt, Cefn Llanfair, Llanfair Road, Llandysul, Ceredigion, Wales, UK, SA44 4RB
www.honorwoodflocks.co.uk

P & M Woolcraft
Pindon End Cottage, Pindon End, Hanslope, Milton Keynes, UK, MK19 7HN
www.pmwoolcraft.co.uk

Riihivilla (Leena Riihela)
Finland www.riihivilla.com

Scottish Fibres
23 Damhead, Lothianburn, Edinburgh, Scotland, UK, EH10 7EA
www.scottishfibres.co.uk

Wild Fibres
Studio 1-135, The Custard Factory, Gibb Street, Birmingham, UK, B9 4AA
www.wildfibres.co.uk

Wingham Wool Work
70 Main Street, Rotherham, South Yorkshire, UK, S62 7BR
www.winghamwoolwork.co.uk

The Woad Centre, Woad Barn, Rawhall Lane, Beetley, Dereham, Norfolk, UK, NR20 4HH
www.thewoadcentre.co.uk

World of Wool, Unit 8, The Old Railway Goods Yard, Scar Lane, Milnsbridge, Huddersfield, West Yorkshire, UK, HD3 4PE
www.worldofwool.co.uk

Dried Herbs

G. Baldwin & Co,
171 – 173 Walworth Road, London, UK, SE17 1RW
www.baldwins.co.uk

Fabrics

Whaleys (Bradford) Ltd, Harris Court, Great Horton, Bradford, West Yorkshire UK, BD7 4EQ
www.whaleys.co.uk

Plants and Seeds

British Wild Flower Plants, Burlingham Gardens, 31 Main Road, North Burlingham, Norfolk, UK, NR13 4TA
www.wildflowers.co.uk

Naturescape, Lapwing Meadows, Coach Gap Lane, Langar, Nottinghamshire, UK, NG13 9HP
www.naturescape.co.uk

Poyntzfield Herb Nursery
Black Isle, By Dingwall, Ross and Cromarty, Scotland, UK, IV7 8LX
www.poyntzfieldherbs.co.uk

Saith Ffynnon Wildlife Plants
Saith Ffynnon Farm, Whitford, Holywell, Flintshire, Wales, UK, CH8 9EQ
www.7wells.co.uk

Acknowledgements

I am grateful to many dyers throughout the world whose work has inspired and informed me over the years and especially to the late Jill Goodwin, whose book *A Dyer's Manual* was such an important source of information and guidance for me and for many other dyers of my generation. Particular thanks go to Finnish expert natural dyer Leena Riihela, who not only shared her knowledge and experience but also supplied me with fungi, lichen and bedstraw roots for my dyeing experiments and kindly allowed me to use some of her photos (see credits below); thanks, too, to India Flint, whose pioneering work in developing the eco-printing and ice-flower techniques introduced me and many other dyers to new and exciting ways of using plants for colour. I am grateful to Michel Garcia for information on the 1-2-3 indigo vat technique and for explaining some details of the chemistry involved and I thank Krista Vajanto of the University of Helsinki for sharing information from her research on the use of buckthorn bark in the Iron Age. My thanks also go to friend, plant expert and fellow dyer, Chris Dobson, who kindly sought out many dye plants for my experiments and shared experiences with me around the dye pots, and to Sue Craig and Dianne Heddy for their assistance with producing some of the dyed samples. I thank also Colin Walton of Walton Creative, who responded so patiently to my frequent queries about photography but who is in no way responsible for any of my shortcomings in that sphere. Thanks, too, to Katie French, Daniel Conway and the staff at Search Press for their assistance and support. Last, but by no means least, I thank my family and especially my husband Roger, for his help with proof-reading and for his constant love, encouragement and support. Any errors are my own and I take full and sole responsibility for them.

Photo credits

I would like to thank the following for the use of their photographs: David Castor (*Quercus robur* page 107), Sue Craig (Celtic dye samples page 11, weld in flower page 109), Garden Organic (*Equisetum arvense* page 70), Leena Riihela (all fungi pages 140–144, *Alnus glutinosa* page 55, *Frangula alnus* page 75, *Solidago canadensis* page 131, *Tanacetum vulgare* page 133), ukwildflowers.com (*Arctostaphylos uva-ursi* page 58, *Epilobium hirsutum* page 69, *Hypericum perforatum* page 84, *Rhamnus cathartica* page 111, *Rubia peregrina* page 116).

All other photos by Jenny and Roger Dean.

Index

silk 21,22,28,29,39,40,
  43,100
soda ash 20,32,35,88,
  92,121,153
sodium carbonate
  (see washing soda)
sodium hydrosulphite
  88,89,94,95
Solidago spp. 131
sorrel 125
Spectralite 89,95
St. John's Wort 84
storing
  dye solutions 8,19,31,
    67,102
  dyestuffs 25,67
  mordant solutions
    8,28,29
  woad solution 101
sweet woodruff 78
sycamore 52

Tanacetum parthenium
  132
Tanacetum vulgare 133
tannin mordant 29
tansy 133
Tapinella atrotomentosa
  141
Taxus baccata 134
Tilia cordata 135
tin 7,16,151
Tyrian purple 136,146,149

Umbilicaria pustulata 136
urine vat
  woad/indigo 92,99

vegetable fibres
  21,22,28,29
vinegar 20,34,35,36,
  40,41,71,100,119
Vikings 30,102,147,148

walnut 23,102,147
  hulls 102
  leaves 102
wash-fastness 18,38
washing 33,38
washing soda 19,20,22,
  32,34,35,88,90
water 20
weld 12,13,16,17,23,
  32,34,109,146
wetting-out 27
wild madder 11,12,116,
  146,147
wild plants 17
willow 29,126
willow herb 69
woad 23,86,146,147
woad balls 93
wood ash water
  12,17,20,32,34,35,121
woodruff 78
wool 14,21,22,29,
  30,33,36,38

Xanthoria parietina 138

yarrow 53
yew 134